Concepts of State, Sovereignty and International Law

With
Special Reference to the
Juristic Conception of the State

By
JOHANNES MATTERN, Ph. D.
The Johns Hopkins University

THE LAWBOOK EXCHANGE, LTD.
Clark, New Jersey

ISBN 978-1-58477-918-6

Lawbook Exchange edition 2008, 2022

The quality of this reprint is equivalent to the quality of the original work.

THE LAWBOOK EXCHANGE, LTD.
33 Terminal Avenue
Clark, New Jersey 07066-1321

Please see our website for a selection of our other publications and fine facsimile reprints of classic works of legal history:
www.lawbookexchange.com

Library of Congress Cataloging-in-Publication Data

Mattern, Johannes, 1882-
Concepts of state, sovereignty, and international law:with special reference to the juristic conception of the state / by Johannes Mattern.
p. cm.
Originally published: Baltimore, Md.: Johns Hopkins Press, 1928.
Includes bibliographical references and index.
ISBN-13: 978-1-58477-918-6 (cloth : alk. paper)
ISBN-10: 1-58477-918-7 (cloth : alk. paper)
1. State, The. 2. Sovereignty. 3. International law. I. Title.
KZ4002.M37 2008
341.26--dc22 2008021275

Printed in the United States of America on acid-free paper

Concepts of State, Sovereignty and International Law

With
Special Reference to the
Juristic Conception of the State

By
JOHANNES MATTERN, Ph. D.
The Johns Hopkins University

1928

THE JOHNS HOPKINS PRESS
Baltimore
Maryland

HUMPHREY MILFORD
Oxford University Press
Amen House, London, E. C. 4

PRESS OF MEYER & THALHEIMER
BALTIMORE, MD., U. S. A.

To
Professor W. W. Willoughby

"....We must realize that, however ancient may be the traditions of maritime law, however diverse the sources from which it has been drawn, it derives its whole and only power in this country from its having been accepted and adopted by the United States. There is no mystic over law to which even the United States must bow. When a case is said to be governed by foreign law or by general maritime law, that is only a short way for saying that, for this purpose, the sovereign power takes up a rule suggested from without, and makes it part of its own rules...."

"Also we must realize that the authority that makes the law is itself superior to it, and that, if it consents to apply to itself the rules that it applies to others, the consent is free and may be withheld. The sovereign does not create justice in an ethical sense, to be sure, and there may be cases in which it would not dare to deny that justice for fear of war or revolution. Sovereignty is a question of power [legal competence], and no human power [competence] is unlimited...." (Mr. Justice Holmes in Western Maid, etc., 257 U. S. 432).

CONTENTS

CHAPTER V

The Austinian or Analytical School

CHAPTER VI

Willoughby's Juristic Conception of the State

CHAPTER VII

Criticism of the Theory

CHAPTER VIII

Vinogradoff's Modification of the Theory

CHAPTER IX

Denial of Sovereignty by Duguit, Laski, and Others

CHAPTER X

The State and the Civitas Maxima According to the Austrian School

CHAPTER XI

German Conception of Sovereignty Without Independence

CHAPTER XII

The Juristic Conception of the State Restated

CHAPTER XIII

General Applicability of the Juristic Conception of the State

PREFACE

In the fall of 1923 the author began to direct his researches to the promising field of the new European constitutions, starting with the constitutional jurisprudence and government of the German National Republic. The fundamental ideas of the new German National Constitution were found to rest squarely upon the juristic conception of the State, a theory ably presented to the English speaking world by Professor W. W. Willoughby.

Confronted in 1924 with the opportunity of offering the results of his examination of the new German Constitution as a course of lectures during Professor Willoughby's absence from The Johns Hopkins University, the author was faced with the necessity of examining to his own and to the student's satisfaction the question of the general applicability and tenability of the juristic conception of the State as an essential prelude to the main subject of the German Constitution erected upon the foundation of this theory.

An inquiry into the general acceptability of the juristic conception of the State could, however, be of value only if carried on by way of a comparative study of other important theories of the State in their bearing upon the development of this particular doctrine.

As a result of this inquiry the present work was first intended to constitute the introductory chapter to the author's "Principles of Constitutional Jurisprudence of the German National Republic." But having outgrown its original proportion it is here, at the urgent request of a number of the students attending the course of lectures referred to, offered in the present form.

In justice to critic and author alike, it must be stated with emphasis that the work as here presented does not pretend to give an exhaustive exposition of the theories of State and Sovereignty. To be more specific, the author does not lay claim to an enlargement of the material knowledge concerning the doctrines analysed in the earlier chapters dealing with Bodin, Hooker, Hobbes, Locke, Rousseau, Kant, Hegel, Fichte, and Austin. He merely aims to offer a more precise and detached valuation of the doctrines of these thinkers in the general economy of political theories and particularly in their bearing upon the juristic conception of the State. In the later chapters dealing with the juristic conception of the State, its criticism and attempted modification, the author offers what he believes to be new and important elements in their bearing upon the juristic conception of the State, hitherto ignored or inadequately treated by American scholars.

J. M.

INTRODUCTION

Conflicting Theories of State and Sovereignty

In the study of a country's system of government as defined in its constitution we have to deal with a number of terms or concepts, the most perplexing of which are those of State and Sovereignty. It is difficult enough to find a generally acceptable definition or thought content of these terms in the consideration of the fundamental law of a single country. In a contemporary study of the constitutions of a number of different States, the task has so far proved practically impossible. However, without the establishment of a generally applicable meaning of these terms the attempt to arrive at an understanding of the constitutional organisms of foreign State systems must appear vain.

The definitions of the terms State and Sovereignty are so intimately connected that we cannot conceive of the one without the other. The State has very broadly been defined as "a society of human individuals viewed as a politically organized unit." [1] But when is such a society to be considered as politically organized? The same authority whose definition of the State has just been cited explains that "when this society becomes organized for the effectuation of certain general or, as they are called, political interests, and with a magistracy into whose hands is entrusted the exercise of its controlling authority, it assumes a political form, and a State is said to exist." [2]

[1] Willoughby, The Juristic Conception of the State (The American Political Science Review, vol. XII, 1918, p. 192).

[2] Willoughby, The Nature of the State, p. 3.

Thus it is not the presence of these so-called political aims or interests, in the group, which alone suffices to transform a social unit into a political organism, but rather in addition to their presence there must be in evidence the successful operation of a system of control, however simple, which assures the realization of these interests for the benefit of the whole group. It is the consciousness of certain common interests in the group and the existence of a system of legally binding control by the group over the individual for the realization of these interests which together constitute the essence of the State.

These general interests and the methods of control have been found to vary in different political organizations of the past and present. In the attempt to define the character of the State and of Sovereignty so as to differentiate these variations, political scientists have come to speak of different kinds of States and offer varying and even contradictory theories of Sovereignty and its location. But in doing so they patently confound essence and form, the universal and the individual. The essential and universal in State and Sovereignty are the presence of certain common interests in the group and the existence of a system of effectual control by the group over the individual for the attainment of these interests. Variation of these interests and of the mode of control in the different groups represents the formal and individual aspect of the matter. Hence these manifold definitions of State and Sovereignty are in reality not theories of the State as a generic concept, but rather descriptions of the particular State organization to which the particular author happens to be attached or favorable. The error is one of failing to distinguish between State and form of government, between the possession of Sovereignty and the act and method of governing.

As such the error is confusing enough, but it becomes hopelessly so when the attempt is carried to the extent of applying any or every one of these different theories to any or all other political systems, no matter how different their historical development or present organization may be. Thus theories are advanced, which are claimed to be definitions of the term State as universal concepts but which in reality are nothing more or less than descriptions of particular State organizations, such as Monarchy,—absolute or constitutional; Republic, Aristocracy, Oligarchy, Democracy; Unitary state, State federation, Federation of States. A difference of form is mistaken for a difference of the *Ding an sich.* In other words political philosophers have fallen into the error of mistaking any one of a number of different constitutional systems for a general theory of the State, or as the Germans term it, *eine allgemeine Staatslehre.*[3]

This error is responsible for most of the differences of opinion on the question of what State and Sovereignty are and where the latter is located. Not until this error is recognized and remedied, or until a definition of the State and of Sovereignty and its location is found, which is so broad and simple that it may be applied consistently to all existing politically organized societies, can we expect to do justice to and to appreciate foreign constitutions and governments. This realization calls for a critical analysis of the most important theories of the State and Sovereignty advanced in the past, first from the point of view of their general applicability to the modern State and second with regard to their bearing upon the juristic conception of the State which forms the starting point of this inquiry.

[3] See in this connection Willoughby, The Fundamental Concepts of Public Law, pp. 11 ff, especially chapter IX.

CHAPTER I

Bodin's Theory of Sovereignty Applied to Contemporary Europe

Bodin's Theory of Sovereignty. The term sovereignty is of French origin, being derived from the French "souverain," meaning excellent, highest, supreme. The French term is derived from the medieval Latin "supranus," the adjective from "super." [1] The term was first used in medieval relations and law, being applied to the chieftains of feudal Europe. Used in this connection it generally was the equivalent of the term prince or *Fürst.* Gradually, however, the term sovereignty in its medieval meaning was applied to every authority which gave a final decision.[2] As the central monarchy in France succeeded in establishing its overlordship over the feudal chieftains it also absorbed, for its own use, the term sovereignty heretofore applied to feudal lords and local administrative bodies.[3] It was the use of the term in this application to the National supreme power or to the authority of the French King, to which the Frenchman Jean Bodin, writing during the reign of Henry III (1551-1589), gave scientific treatment. He thus attempted to justify in the domain of law, philosophy and morals, that rule of absolutism which alone had made it possible for the French kings of the 14th and 15th centuries to create the united Kingdom of France or the united French Nation by the gradual extension of royal suzerainty over the feudal lords of the realm.

[1] Du Cange, Glossarium Mediae et Infimae Latinitatis.

[2] See Lieber, Political Ethics, vol. I, p. 245 ff.

[3] *Ibidem.*

Bodin's conception of Sovereignty and its location has been excellently stated in Bullowa's "History of the Theory of Sovereignty," from which the following quotations are offered:

"The fundamental proposition of Bodin is that in every independent community governed by law there must be some authority whereby the laws themselves are established, and which must, therefore, be above them; some power to which all other powers of the State are subject, and which itself is subject to none. This authority, possessing absolute power, is sovereign, and is the test of an independent State.

"Sovereignty is the most high, absolute and perpetual power over citizens and subjects in a State, itself not subject to the laws, but maker and master of them. The supreme power cannot be subject to control or condition, since who could limit it and not be himself sovereign? It can neither be delegated nor alienated in part, since its very nature will not permit of partition. Is not, then, the greatest sovereign subject to the laws of God and of nature? As an individual a sovereign prince cannot abrogate these [laws] without committing high treason against heaven, but he is answerable to Almighty God alone, and his subjects have no lawful power to condemn him. Neither the laws of nations nor those of his own predecessors are binding upon a sovereign. He is bound only in moral duty and in honor by his conventions with other princes and with his own subjects. . .

"The power to give laws to all subjects in general without the consent of anyone is the chief mark of sovereignty. He who receives law or orders from another by force or by contract is in nowise sovereign. . .

"Monarchy, aristocracy and democracy are states in which one [individual], a minority, or a majority exercises sovereignty; no mixed state is possible, as sovereignty is by its nature indivisible. . ."[4]

There can certainly be no denial of the fact that this theory of Sovereignty was nothing short of a description in philosophical or juristic language, of the absolute power possessed by the kings of France at the period of Bodin's writing and for more than a century preceding his time. For, though admitting that the existing States include Monarchies, Aristocracies and Democracies in which Sovereignty is exercised respectively by one individual, by a minority or a majority, Bodin holds, nevertheless, that in the ideal system the king or prince alone is vested with the supreme power called sovereignty[5] and this supreme authority he possesses by divine right.

"Since there is next to God nothing greater on earth than sovereign princes," so Bodin writes, "and since they have been established by Him as His lieutenants, to command the rest of men (aux autres hommes) regard must

[4] Bullowa, pp. 27-29. Bullowa's references to Bodin are to the De Republica, Francofurti, 1641; tr. by Thomas Knolles. The text consulted by the author is that of the French edition: Les six livres de la République....à Genève par Etienne Gamonet, 1629.

[5] "We have shown the intolerable absurdities which would follow if the vassals were sovereign, even if they are in no dependence upon some one else and how this would be equivalent to placing on the same level the lord and the subject, the master and the servant, him who gives the law and him who receives it, him who commands with him who obeys. Since this is impossible, it must be concluded that dukes, counts, and all those who are in dependence on some other, or who receive laws or commandments from another, be it by force or by obligation, are not sovereign. And we even judge of the greatest magistrates, lieutenants, generals of kings, governors, regents, dictators, whatever their powers be, that if they are obligated by the laws, the jurisdiction and commandment of another, they are not sovereign. For the marks of sovereignty are becoming only to a sovereign prince." (Bodin, Les Six Livres de la République, p. 214).

be had of their quality, so to respect and revere their majesty in complete obedience, to think (sentir) and speak of them in all honor, for who despises His sovereign prince, despises God whose image he [the prince] is." [6]

The question naturally presents itself as to why, if the French kings of his period and of long generations preceding his time actually possessed this supreme authority, Bodin considered it necessary to write his voluminous treatise on a subject whose practical aspects had been and were well known and understood in his own country. Bodin himself gives at least a formal answer to this question. "It is necessary," so he says, "here to form a definition of sovereignty because no jurist nor political philosopher has defined the same, though it is the principal and most necessary point to be understood in the treatment of the State (de la République)." [7]

Though in this answer Bodin apparently claims for his theory of Sovereignty a general juristic and philosophical validity, his conception of the supreme power of the sovereign prince is nothing more than a technical formulation of the constitutional theories upon which the French monarchy of his time was built, or stated inversely, it is the formulation of a constitutional theory evolved from the existing system of French monarchism.[8] This be-

[6] *Ibid.* pp. 211-212, see also p. 270.

[7] *Ibid.* p. 122.

[8] Though Bodin makes his theory of Sovereignty a mere part, however essential, of his system of the State, and thus at least nominally assigns to it a place rather detached from the background of the politico-religious controversy then raging between the *monarchomachi* and the adherents of the divine right theory in England and between the regalists and the Ligueurs, the Politiques and the ultramontanists in France, a general historical study of the theory of Sovereignty could, of course, not limit itself to a consideration of Bodin's theory apart from these settings. For the present work, however, such a general study is not required. For a general treatment of the kind mentioned above see Figgis, The Divine Right of Kings, and his Studies of Political thought from Gerson to Grotius, 1414-1625.

comes all the more evident when we consider that two hundred years later, with completely changed political and social conditions, we see a new and radically different theory of State and Sovereignty advanced by the political writers and actors of the French Revolution.

Sovereignty in the Holy Roman Empire. Another factor disproving the general character of Bodin's theory is to be found in the consideration of the political and constitutional system of France's eastern neighbor, the Holy Roman Empire of the German Nation. While in France the political development during the 14th and 15th centuries had been favorable to the formulation of a legal and philosophical conception of an absolute power in the possession of the king, the situation in the Holy Roman Empire of the German Nation was taking a turn in a different direction. The rigid Roman conception of imperial *majestas* and *dominium* was ill suited to the individualistic character and particularist tendencies of the German political and racial groups.[9] Accepting the heritage of the Roman Imperium from the hands of the Papacy the German kings failed to realize the dangers of the bonds attached to the gift,—bonds which were to prove fatal to the exercise of the majestas at the very time when all their authority and freedom of action was required in the struggle with the princes of the Empire to whom they owed their election and upon whom they remained dependent for the possession of their office of *Princeps principum.* In turn, this inability to assert their imperial authority over refractory and rebellious electors and princes was a serious handicap in their attempt to resist the political overlord-

[9] A more detailed consideration of this phase will be found in the author's Principles of Constitutional Jurisprudence of the German National Republic, chapter I.

ship which the Papacy asserted over those whom it had anointed emperors of Rome.

Surely to such conditions or to such a political system Bodin's definition of Sovereignty could not apply. If there was in this dual body politic any successful claim to supreme authority it must be sought not in the power of the Emperor over the princes of the component States of the Reich, but rather in the rule of the individual princes over their own subjects within the geographical limits of their particular electorates or principalities. In the adoption of the principle of *cuius regio, eius religio,* this local absolutism received its moral and legal sanction in the Treaty of Augsburg in 1555. In the Treaty of Muenster of 1648, ending the Thirty Years' War, the principle of local Sovereignty gained its legal recognition and final victory over the idea of imperial authority or suzerainty.

Bodin's State was the National State, his Sovereignty the unquestionable and unquestioned supremacy of the king of this National State over all other claimants of political power within the realm. For all practical purposes, and after 1648 in constitutional and international law, the sovereign State in the Holy Roman Empire of the German Nation was not the Empire, but each one of the individual principalities of which the Empire was formed. From the sixteenth century to the dissolution of the Empire in 1806 the actual sovereigns were the rulers of these component parts, bidding defiance to imperial authority and preventing national unity in the sense in which this had been established in France.[10]

[10] In the consideration of the modern German conception of Sovereignty we shall find that Germany's leading philosophers and publicists have accepted and extolled the idea of the National State and Bodin's theory of Sovereignty as a supreme power of National scope, but that the same particularist tendencies which prevented the victory of the National idea in the Medieval Empire also proved the stumbling block in the efforts of Germany's statesmen to realize this idea in the creation of the Empire in 1871 and of the Republic in 1919.

Bodin's Influence in England. Shortly after its publication Bodin's treatise on the State and Sovereignty was introduced into the lecture rooms of Cambridge. It was received as a welcome aid by the adherents of the theory of the divine right of kings in their fight against the onslaught of the *monarchomachi.* In asserting its claim to temporal supremacy over all earthly potentates the Papacy had come into conflict not only with the rulers of the Holy Roman Empire, but also with the new National States which were arising from the ruins of feudalism in France and England. Discussing the influence of the writings of Wycliffe upon Richard II of England, John N. Figgis calls attention to the fact that ever "from the time of Edward I, who outlawed the clergy rather than submit to the bull *clericis laicos,* there had been passed a series of statutes in restraint of Papal claims," and he thinks that "all this might well induce a writer with an anticlerical bias or a monarch with high ideas of his own dignity, to claim complete 'freedom,' i. e., sovereignty for the English Crown, and to claim it as coming by Divine Right." [11] It was for this reason that long before the continental Reformation England produced, in the works of Ockham, Wycliffe and others, a strong defense of regal against papal supremacy. It was natural, then, that the Reformation, when it came, gave to the Tudor dynasty a tremendous increase of power and that political writers of the time should develop the doctrine of the divine right of kings as the rock of England's existence as an independent National State whose independence seemed threatened by the claims of the Papacy from without, by the writings of the *monarchomachi* and the theory and practice of resistance, active and passive, on the parts of the religious non-

[11] Figgis, The Divine Right of Kings, pp. 66-67.

conformists from within.[12] However, once the battle for English religious and political security was won, the idea of the divine right of kings, having accomplished its mission, was cast by the wayside in favor of parliamentary supremacy [13] and a theory of national or rather parliamentary Sovereignty as finally crystallized and defined by Austin and the Austinian School.[14]

[12] See note 8.

[13] *Ibid.*

[14] See chapter V (Austin's Theory of Law and Sovereignty).

CHAPTER II

THE COMPACT THEORY OF HOOKER, HOBBES, LOCKE AND ROUSSEAU

The Origin of the Theory. Between the time of Bodin's definition of Sovereignty and the development of Austin's theory, the French Revolution had taken place. While this event is generally held to have given birth to what is called the theory of popular Sovereignty, it in fact merely put into practice a theory which in principle goes back to Roman and feudal law. According to Roman juristic theory the people are supposed to have surrendered, by the fiction of an original compact with their rulers, their rights and power into the keeping and to the management of the prince, king, emperor, magistrate or assembly. This surrender was held to be entire and irrevocable.[1] In the feudal system the legal basis of the relations between lord

[1] The phrase: Quod principi placuit, legis habet vigorem (Justinian, Inst. I. 2. 6), to be rightly understood must be considered in connection with the statement immediately following: Cum lege regia quae de imperio ejus lata est, populus ei et in eum omne suum imperium et potestatem concessit (The ordinance of the prince has the force of a law, for the people by the *lex regia* have made a concession to him of their whole power). Hence the same Roman legal system could define law as "what the Roman people enact at the request of a senatorial magistrate" (Lex est, quod populus Romanus senatorio magistratu interrogante, veluti consule, constituebat) (Justinian, Inst. I. 2. 4.), or as Gaius in his Institutiones (I. 1. 3.) expresses it: Lex est quod populus jubet atque constituit (A Law is that which the people decree and establish); and (*Ibid.*, I. 1. 5.): Constitutio principis est quod imperator decreto vel edicto vel epistula constituit, nec nunquam dubitatum est quin id legis vicem obtineat cum ipse imperator per legem imperium accipiat. (A constitution is law established by the emperor either by decree, edict or letter; and it has never been doubted that this has the force of law (statute), since the emperor himself receives his authority by law (statute). See Willoughby, The Political Theories of the Ancient World, chapter XVI.

and vassal was a contract which was not fictitious but historical and real. This feudal contract was not irrevocable. Its validity depended entirely on the faithful execution of the terms agreed upon by the two parties concerned. The failure of the one party to live up to the conditions of the contract would legally release the other from his obligations towards the party in default.[2]

It was largely under the influence of this system of the mutually binding force of the feudal contract that the Roman conception of the irrevocable character of the people's surrender of their rights to the ruler was modified by early Christian and medieval writers. As it was thus modified this governmental pact was considered to effect "nothing more than a delegation of power to the rulers, such power to be used by them only for the purposes for which granted, and liable to be recalled upon being misused."[3]

The Christian conception of the State as applied to the Holy Roman Empire of the German Nation was one that

[2] Concerning the character of the feudal contract Sir Henry Maine writes as follows: "The earliest feudal communities were neither bound together by mere sentiment nor recruited by a fiction. The tie which united them was a Contract, and they obtained new associates by contracting with them. The relations of lord to the vassals had originally been settled by express engagement, and a person wishing to engraft himself in the brotherhood by *commendation* or *infeudation* came to a distinct understanding as to the conditions on which he was to be admitted. It is therefore the sphere occupied in them by contract which principally distinguishes the feudal institutions from unadulterated usages of primitive races. The lord had many of the characteristics of a patriarchal chieftain, but his prerogative was limited by a variety of settled customs traceable to the express conditions which had been agreed upon when the infeudation took place." (Ancient Law, p. 353).

[3] See Willoughby, The Nature of the State, p. 59. The rôle which the doctrine of the superiority of divine and natural law over man made law played in this connection will be referred to later.

could not be dissociated from the conception of the Church itself. Both Church and State were conceived as being of divine origin. Christ was their universal head, the Pope his earthly representative in the spiritual field, the Emperor in the sphere of purely mundane affairs. Both were apparently to be on a plane of equality before their heavenly Lord, but as matters developed, this assumed equality remained unquestioned only so long as Pope and Emperor were in agreement. As soon as they differed in the exercise of their respective competencies Christ's vicar in the sphere of the spiritual claimed and asserted from the days of Gregory VII onward the superiority of the Spiritual Power over the rulers of the mundane.[4] It was in the struggle thus ensuing between these two forces that the compact theory either in the original Roman or the modified feudal form, as expediency required, was appealed to by the adherents of both sides. By the imperial apologists it was resorted to in order to prove the Emperor's independence of papal political control or Sovereignty. But such an appeal was apt to prove effective only so long as people and emperor were at one. This fact was quickly grasped by the papal followers who on the basis of the supposed contractual relations of emperor and subjects asserted the right of popular resistence in the struggle between popes and emperors. After the Reformation both Catholic and Protestant writers attempted to justify on the same principle the right of popular resistance to interference on the part of the princes with the religion of their subjects. Thus the idea of the compact or contract and the resulting idea of popular Sovereignty were transferred from the sphere of jurisprudence and philosophy to the

[4] On the subject of the medieval relation of the papal and worldly powers see Gierke, Political Theories of the Middle Ages. . . tr. by Maitland. . . .Cambridge, 1913; also the two works of Figgis cited.

battle grounds of these political religious feuds. In consequence it received considerable publicity but, as a political or constitutional doctrine, it made no appreciable progress until by the endeavors of Hooker, Hobbes, Locke and Rousseau, the subject was at least in theory reestablished as a problem of philosophical and political speculation.

But though the efforts of these writers secured the liberation of the subject of popular Sovereignty, as implied in the various concepts of the compact theory, from its position as a mere pawn in the game of partisan religious and political controversy, the doctrine nevertheless remained most intimately connected with the attempt to offer an immediate and effective solution of the political and constitutional difficulties of the countries and periods concerned.

Hooker. It is an important, though little known fact, that the theories of Hooker, Hobbes, Locke and Rousseau were the result of their personal concern over the religious and political struggles taking place at their time in the countries to which they owed allegiance or where they found asylum and domicile. As pointed out by Professor Willoughby, Hooker's consideration of the State and Sovereignty was merely incidental. In his "Ecclesiastical Polity," published in 1594, he proposed to justify the established Church of England "by denying that the Church was necessarily subject to divine regulation in all matters," and asserting "that for its government laws might be made by men, so long as they were not contrary to the Scriptures." Thus "he was led to an inquiry regarding the origin of all authority" which "he found in the consent of the governed." Assuming a state of lawlessness and war as a pre-civic condition of man, Hooker posited the social compact as an escape from this state. He did not follow out to its various consequences the theory thus advanced, but left this task to his successors, Hobbes, Locke, and Rousseau.[5]

Hobbes. Though Hobbes spent many years abroad, he was keenly interested in the political unrest following the events of 1628 and 1629. When he returned to England in 1637 he had ready what he called "a little treatise in English," in which he sought to show that the points of the royal prerogatives which the members of Parliament were determined to dispute, before granting the supplies asked, "were inseparably annexed to the sovereignty which they did not then deny to be in the King." When in 1642 civil war broke out and the King's cause began to decline Hobbes was one of the first of the political refugees to leave England for France. The sufferings of the fugitive royalists prompted the writing and publication of the *De Cive* and the *Leviathan* in which he undertook to set forth his whole theory of government based upon his experiences during the political upheavals of the England of his time.

The Leviathan which appeared in 1651 contained as a closing chapter a general review of the political situation. The King being dead, Hobbes in this survey raised the question of the right of the citizen to change his allegiance when the former sovereign power had ceased to accord the protection for which the individual was supposed to have surrendered his natural right of existence and self-defense. Thus the Leviathan was hailed by some as a glorification of the Commonwealth of Cromwell. On the other hand it lost Hobbes the confidence of his exiled royalist friends and the protection of the French government without gaining him the good will of the liberals at home.[6]

[5] Willoughby, Nature of the State, pp. 62-63.

[6] Encyclopedia Britannica, Hobbes.

According to Hobbes the state of Society prior to the creation of government was one of war. There were only the natural rights of self protection and liberty, based upon reason and utility. In order that all might gain greater protection and security each individual agreed with the other to give up part of their individual and natural rights to one man or body of men to govern them all and secure thus greater protection by the strength of all.

Hobbes held the State was established by a contract, not between Society, considered as a body, and the ruler, but by a covenant between each individual member of Society with every other, to the effect that each individually, not contracted, but surrendered to one man or a body of men, his individual right to govern himself, on the condition that every other member of the Society would do likewise.

The multitude thus united in the one man or group of men as their governor, is called the Commonwealth, the great Leviathan. The united wills of the individuals of the Commonwealth to be thus all governed by their chosen ruler instead of each by himself constitute the sovereign will of the Commonwealth. Sovereignty thus willed is the authority to govern over all. The governor, one or many, is the Sovereign and said to have sovereign powers. Every one besides the governor is his subject. The commands of the sovereign governing power are legally binding upon the members of the Commonwealth regardless of their effect upon the individual or the group. They constitute civil law as distinct from natural law which had been the only restraining element of the pre-civic state of Society.

The right of the Sovereign to rule as indicated above was not a subject of contract between Society, or individual, and the ruler, but the result of a voluntary surrender by each individual of his natural right to govern himself. Hence there can be no breach of covenant on the part of the ruler, for the reason that he is not a party to any covenant. Sovereignty thus acquired by the ruler is therefore irrevocable and any lawful absolution of the subject from obedience to the Sovereign impossible. Actual release takes place only when the Sovereign ceases to govern and Society thus returns to the non-political state of anarchy and war.

Effecting the individual surrender of the right of self-government directly to the ruler, Hobbes failed to distinguish between the political organization of the Commonwealth and the institution of the ruler, i. e. between State and Government. Hence he identified the failure of the ruler to govern with the end of the Society as a body politic.

Locke. Poor health and ill-favor of the Stuarts forced Locke to spend more than twelve years in France and Holland. He did not return to England until after the revolution of 1688. His Two Treatises on Civil Government, published in 1690, were intended to aid in the solution of the struggle between the theory of the divine right of kings and the principle of democracy. They "were meant to vindicate the Convention parliament and the English revolution, as well as to refute the ideas of absolute monarchy held by Hobbes and Filmer."[7] Thus Locke, too, conceived his system under the influence of the political turmoil of his time.

The pre-civic state of nature was conceived by Locke as one, not of war and anarchy, but of natural equality and freedom. In this state the individual was endowed with certain natural rights, such as the rights of property and

[7] *Ibid.*, Locke.

self-defense. It was for the preservation and better enjoyment of these rights that every individual entered into a compact with the rest of the group, by which he surrendered the exercise of part of his natural rights to the general authority of the group. But the condition of the compact was, that by the surrender of the exercise of part of his rights he should secure the protection and preservation of his remaining rights by the public authority to be instituted by Society. Thus the individual, according to Locke entered into a contract with Society for the better government and greater security of his natural rights and interests.

There seems to be in Locke's theory of the creation of the State a realization of the difference between Society as body politic and Government as the agent of this body. It is Society as a political organization which assumes responsibility for the preservation of the rights of its members. Government, or in this case the legislative, is instituted by this Society, thus organized, for the definite purpose of exercising the latter's authority.

In Hobbes' conception of the state of nature the individual was possessed of natural rights, but there was no actual binding law forcing each member of the group to respect the natural rights of the other. In order to escape this existing state of anarchy each member agreed with the other to sacrifice his rights and submit to the control of a ruler expected to give protection to all from each other. The ruler's commands thus became the law of the body politic, or the civil law of the State.

In the state of nature as conceived by Locke, the individual was bound by the law of nature, speaking to him through his reason, not to harm another's life, liberty and property. He was thus morally held to govern himself accordingly. By the surrender of the individual's exercise of the law of nature to the body politic the latter assumed the authority and responsibility of governing all by the same law. The political Society in turn entrusted this governance to the legislative, which thus based its right of enforcement upon the control of the law of nature. However, as the law of nature was held to be binding not only upon the individual but also upon the ruler, the legislative was of course bound to apply natural law for the preservation of the natural rights of the individuals. Hence the legislative had no unlimited power over the members of the group. It was limited by the natural rights still retained by them. If the legislative abused its authority or attempted to assume an absolute power over the lives, liberty and property of the individual, the people were supposed to regain their original liberty of disposing of the delinquent government and of choosing a new legislative to govern the members of the group "for their own safety and security which is the end for which they are in Society."

Here again, as in the conception of the creation of the State, Locke made a distinction between State and Government. But he did not draw from this difference the necessary conclusions. His failure to differentiate between natural and civil law prevented him from positing for the body politic, i. e., the State, a sovereign will in the form of a civil law by which the members of the State as well as the legislative were to be bound. It further prevented him from realizing that the power to remove or alter a legislative acting contrary to the trust imposed upon it, did not rest with the people as members of the social group, but with Society organized as a body politic, i. e., as a State.

Rousseau. The facts of Rousseau's personal interest in the political and social condition of France and Europe of his time and the admitted reformatory object of his writings are too well known to require more than a mere mention in this connection. The limitation of the power of Government not by moral but by legal criteria is probably the most important feature of Rousseau's contribution to the system of the State. In the non-political condition man had his natural liberties of life and property. In order to secure for his freedom a greater protection than he himself could afford to give, each member of the group united with the other in what Rousseau calls the social contract, to form a body politic. This contract is not a compact between the people and the ruler. As explicitly stated by Rousseau: "Those who contend that the act by which the people submit to chiefs is not a contract, are quite right. It is absolutely only a commission, in which, as simple officers of the sovereign, they [the chiefs] exercise in his name the power of which he has made them the depository, and which he can limit, modify and take away as he wishes." [8]

By this contract, which should more fittingly be called political than social, the individual gave into the hands of the State his personal liberty to have it returned to him as a member of the State. The individual wills of the members of the group thus united constitute the general will as the sovereign law of organized society. This general sovereign will can be exercise only by the sovereign people as members of the State. The Government acts only as the executive agent of the popular assembly which alone represents and expresses the will of the sovereign people. According to Rousseau the Government is "an intermediate

[8] Rousseau, Contrat Social, book III, chap. I. See also Willoughby, Nature of the State, pp. 80-81.

body established between subjects and sovereign for their mutual intercourse, charged with the execution of the laws and the maintenance of liberty—civil as well as political. . ." [9] Rousseau carries this difference between Government and the State to such an extent as to hold that when the popular assembly is in session the Government should cease to function. "The instant that the people is legitimately assembled in a sovereign body, all jurisdiction of government ceases." [10]

Rousseau's system is of course impossible of application except in a small city state. As such it has no claim to be considered as a generally acceptable conception of the State and Sovereignty. Its actual interest lies in the fact that his extreme conception of popular Sovereignty is nothing but the natural reaction to Bodin's theory of the absolute sovereign power of the personal Monarch and the actual realization of this system in the government of the French Monarchy at whose Capital Rousseau wrote the "Contrat Social."

Theories of Government, not of State. It is the immediacy of interest on the part of these writers in the practical aspect of the political struggles of their times and of their particular countries, and above all the fact that in this struggle they openly sponsored different and opposing principles, which deprived their theories of State and Sovereignty of the aspect of universality indispensible to their general application and acceptance. In fact, the brief analysis of their theories offered in the preceding pages shows beyond a doubt that their doctrines, far from being theories of the State as a general concept, on the contrary, are philosophical definitions of methods of con-

[9] Rousseau, *Ibid.*
[10] *Ibid.*, chapter XIV.

trol suitable to the form of State of their particular choosing. They are theories of Government, not of State. What has been said here of Hooker, Hobbes, Locke and Rosseau, applies to a large extent also to Althusius, Grotius and to the German political philosophers of the early nineteenth century, Kant, Hegel and Fichte, whose doctrines will be considered later.

This interpretation of the political writings of the centuries in question finds corroboration in Alfred Weber's recent work dealing with the crisis of the modern idea of the State in Europe. "All these works....," so Weber writes, "originated—as already alluded to by Ranke—as writings of an opportunist and polemical character, with a purely practical point of view, employing the ideas and concepts of the time for quite definite purposes. Bodin wrote in favor of the absolute king against the French états; Grotius in favor of freedom of Dutch commerce and traffic against the arbitrary seizures and piracy of the Portuguese and others; Althusius in favor of the old liberties of East Frisia, apparently stimulated by the struggle for liberation then going on in the Netherlands; Hobbes, applied in 1651 the newly acquired individualistic concepts of the political structure in the elaboration of a peculiarly rationalistic base for a sovereign absolutism (der absolutistischen Staatsgewalt), in open combat against the first real democratic European tendency of the levellers; while Locke's Treatises on Government, which had almost acquired the character of canonical importance, represent in certain measure the final reconciling reasoning of the great English Revolution embodying the conclusion drawn from all the positions [of contemporaries and predecessors]. At any rate, in the restless confusion of forces, in the counterplay of power against power; of the ideas of power, faith and class, the concept of the State has, up to the 18th century, always been lagging behind the events. Reflecting, like their shadow, certain intellectual, social and political factors of power. . . , and reconstructing the essentials of the State and thus strengthening one position or the other, the concept of the State did not posit and establish the State as an entity out of a free and original will and within self sufficient norms. . . ." [11]

[11] Weber, Alfred, Die Krise des modernen Staatsgedankens in Europa. . . 1925, pp. 29-30.

CHAPTER III

National and Popular Sovereignty

The Origin of the Theory. The theory of popular Sovereignty, the modern pretender to the place held by the ancient Greek concept of practical democracy, owes its existence, strange as it may seem, to the medieval struggle between the spiritual and mundane rulers for political supremacy in the universal empire. As pointed out above, the Roman idea of the original political compact between people and rulers was one to the effect that the people had surrendered their sovereign right to govern themselves. This surrender was conceived as having been effected without condition and reservation and was thus considered as irrevocable. It was only in case of a vacancy in the office of the ruler that the original Sovereignty was considered as reverting to the people. This reversion (*escheat*) might be held to take place at the natural death of every individual ruler, in which case we are dealing with the election system as prevalent in the Germanic nations, or it might be held to apply only at the extinction of a dynasty, i. e., where hereditary rule obtains. On the other hand there was no room for doubt concerning the mutually obligatory character of the feudal contract as an agreement between lord and vassal entered into by the parties concerned for their respective protection and benefit.

Positing the supremacy of natural, or divine law over man-made law, i. e. the law of the King, the defenders of the Pope's pretensions to political as well as spiritual supremacy came to interpret the political compact on the basis of the monarch's subjectivity to the law of nature, and the voidance of this contract by the monarch's infraction of this supreme law. But once this contract was considered as void, the people as the second part to the agreement had to be conceived as being once more in the possession of their original sovereign right of governing themselves or of choosing their new rulers. Applied in actual practice, this interpretation of the political compact led to repeated demands of the Roman Pontiff for the withdrawal of political allegiance and obedience of the entire body of subjects of refractory kings and emperors, i. e. of kings and emperors offending against the supreme law of nature as interpreted by the Pope and his legal advisors. By a slight confusion of the elements of cause and effect it was only a short and natural step from this refusal of obedience at the bidding of the vicar of Christ to one by way of the people's own volition. For what was more human than the conclusion that if the Pope could bring a king to terms by forcing a whole people into rebellion, the same people could on their own initiative and by the same means compel their rulers to obey the law of nature as interpreted by the people or their accepted leaders.

In this sense the doctrine was applied in the so-called *translatio imperii,* i. e. in the transfer of the Roman Imperium from the Greek to the German Nation. The Greek Emperor having for cause forfeited the Imperium, the latter was held to have reverted to the Roman people who thus were once more free to bestow the same as they might see fit. As stated by Gierke, "therefore the *consensus populi,* which is mentioned on the occasion of Charles the Great's coronation, was the true act of transfer, and the Pope merely declared and executed the will of the people."[1]

[1] Gierke, Political Theories of the Middle Ages, p. 41 ff.

In the same sense the doctrine was resorted to in the political struggle between the *monarchomachi* and the adherents of the theory of the divine right of kings in England and France and in the religious contests between the non-conformists and the advocates of the prince's right to dictate the religious belief of his subjects. The same doctrine was furthermore found serviceable in the issue between the forces contending for the control over the territorial existence and integrity of the realm as illustrated by the popular reaction in the France of the 14th century to the King's willingness in 1344 to sign a treaty providing for the surrender to England of the French duchy of Aquitania (Guyenne). Discussing this proposed surrender, the French cardinals meeting in Avignon expressed themselves to the effect that: "It did not seem possible to them that the Duchy of Aquitania could thus be separated from the crown of France and be assigned to the King of England....because even if the King of France were willing to give his consent, the realm (*regnum*) nevertheless would object nor would it permit that the property of the crown be thus divided, which from antiquity was together (*integra*), nor would the people (*gentes*) nor the community of the said duchy permit that such be done, who did not wish to be subjected to one so much different from themselves." [2]

It is clear, then, that to the extent to which the doctrine of reversion or *escheat* has thus been applied on the one hand for the realization of the will or assumed rights of the people as opposed to that of the ruler, and on the other hand for the maintenance of national solidarity or territorial integrity as opposed to the interests of the dynasty or its individual representative, we must recognize

[2] E. Solière, Le Plébiscite dans l'annexion, pp. 15-16.

in it the seeds of our modern theory of popular and national Sovereignty.

National Sovereignty. The next mile stone in the development of the contract theory, which now had come to be known as the doctrine of popular Sovereignty, was reached in its practical application in the instruments embodying the constitutional legal principles of the new Commonwealth formed by the American Colonies and those of revolutionary France.

The compact theory, and, as the corollary of this doctrine, the theory of man's natural rights, were recognized in the preamble to the American Declaration of Independence and they were explicitly accepted in nearly all of the Bills of Rights of the Constitutions of the various Commonwealths.[3] However, the framers of the Declaration and of the Constitutions concerned subscribed to these theories not because they seemed to be universally acceptable, but because to them they seemed to justify the posi-

[3] The framers of the American Declaration of Independence and the fathers of the Constitution accepted the theory of the political compact as the foundation of liberal or democratic government. As Professor Willoughby states in The Nature of the State: "The compact theory is recognized in the preamble of the Declaration of Independence, and is explicitly accepted in nearly all of the Bills of Rights of the Constitutions of the various commonwealths." Thus the Constitution of New Hampshire declared that: "All men are born equally free and independent. Therefore all government of right originates from the people, is founded in consent, and instituted for the general good." In the preamble to the Constitution of Massachusetts it is said that: "The body politic is formed by a voluntary association of individuals. It is a social compact, by which the whole people covenants with each citizen, and each citizen with the whole people, that all shall be governed by certain laws for the general good." To what impossible extremes the application of this theory will lead when carried to its logical consequences must appear from the views of Jefferson and Madison concerning the period of the validity of this compact. As stated by Willoughby: "Jefferson goes to the extent of

tion which was assumed with regard to their one-time sovereign and ruler.

A similar reason had prevailed upon the authors of the "Declaration of the Rights of Man and Citizen" and of the early Constitutions of revolutionary France. But in this connection we must distinguish between the terms national and popular Sovereignty and the different sense in which they are used.

As we remember, Bodin had posited the supreme sovereign power of the prince as the ideal ruler of the State. It was the actual claim not only to the exercise but also to the possession of the sovereign power by the French kings and their inept or abusive application of that power which had led a Rousseau to the other extreme. Sovereignty, so he taught, belonged to the people and could be exercised only by the people. The Government was the manager rather than the representative agent. A middle ground between these two extreme positions was taken by the framers of the Declaration of the Rights of Man and Citizen and of the Constitution of 1791. Neither the Declaration nor the Constitution denied the French king

holding that one generation cannot bind another, and, based upon a calculation as to the average length of life, says, 'every constitution then, and every law naturally expires at the end of thirty-four years.' At a later date he reduces this period to nineteen years, thus making the natural life of political States, as some one has said, shorter than that of a horse. Madison . . . while not accepting this deduction . . . maintains the contractual origin of political society, and asserts that the continued validity of constitutions and laws rests upon tacit acceptance through the fact of their not being explicitly revoked" (Willoughby, Nature of the State, pp. 87-88). It is the same compact theory which, applied to inter-State relations, led to the States rights theory, the doctrine of nullification and secession, and which met with final disqualification as a result of the American Civil War.

the right to rule, i. e. to exercise the sovereign power, but they did deny him the possession of Sovereignty. They claimed the possession of Sovereignty for the French Nation. King, legislature and judiciary were declared to be the governing agents, and as such only parts, of the Nation.

Thus Article 3 of the Declaration states that: "The foundation (le principe) of all sovereignty resides essentially in the Nation. No single body, no individual can exercise any authority which does not expressly emanate from it [the Nation]."

Articles 1 and 2, Titre III of the Constitution explain that: "Sovereignty is one, indivisible, inalienable and imprescribable; it belongs to the Nation, no section of the people nor any individual can attribute sovereignty to itself or to himself," and that: "The Nation, from which alone all powers (tous les pouvoirs) emanate, can not exercise them except by delegation. The French Constitution is representative: the representatives are the legislative body and the King."

In Articles 3-5 it states that: "The legislative power is delegated to a National Assembly, composed of temporary representatives.... The Government is monarchical; the executive power is delegated to the King, to be exercised under his authority.... The judicial power is delegated to the judges elected by the people...."

The term Nation as here employed clearly implies the totality of the French people not as a social, but as a political organism, i. e. as the French State. The constitutional provision claiming Sovereignty as the attribute of the French Nation by whom the powers of government were delegated to king, legislature and judiciary, implied a political and legal challenge of the theory of the absolute sovereign king expressed in the words attributed to Louis XIV: L'état c'est moi." [4]

Popular Sovereignty. The Constitution of 1793 was intended to be the first constitution of republican France. In its definition of political organization and in its conception of Sovereignty it leaned strongly upon Rousseau. Concerning the object of the social or political compact it said: "The social guarantee consists of the action of all, to assure to every one the enjoyment and the conservation of his rights. This guarantee reposes in the national sovereignty." Defining the location of Sovereignty it stated: "Sovereignty resides in the people: it is one and indivisible, imprescribable and inalienable." [5]

Unlike the Constitution of 1791 the proposed fundamental law of 1793 did not speak of any delegation of the governing power. In fact, very much like Rousseau's idea of a direct government by popular assembly, the framers of the Constitution of 1793 seemed to contemplate a constitutional system in which the political will of the people was to manifest itself in primary conventions only, and in which this will was to be absolutely binding upon the people's mandatories conducting the affairs of the Government.

Thus, for instance, it was provided that:

"No portion of the people can exercise the power of the entire people, but each section of the sovereign in assembly convened, shall enjoy the right of expressing its will with complete liberty.

[4] On the subject of national as distinguished from popular Sovereignty see Malberg, Contribution à la théorie générale de l'état, vol. II, p. 167 ff. Also Willoughby, Fundamental Concepts of Public Law, p. 114 ff.

[5] Declaration of the rights of man and citizen, 1793, Articles 23, 25.

"Any individual usurping sovereignty shall be instantly put to death by free men (hommes libres)."

"Every citizen has an equal right to concur in the formation of the law, the nomination of his mandatories or agents."

"The defaults of the mandatories and the agent of the people shall never go unpunished. No one has the right to consider himself more inviolable than any other citizen." [6]

It is this conception of the individuals forming the Government not as representatives, but as mandatories, absolutely bound by the orders of the sovereign people, which of necessity leads to the resort of revolution when the agents ignore their mandates and thus usurp for themselves sovereign rights, a conclusion which with more logic than practical sense was embodied in the proposed fundamental law of 1793, to the effect that: "When the government violates the right (droit) of the people, insurrection is the most sacred and the most indispensable of duties for the people and for each section (portion) of the people." [7]

The fact that the right of revolution was claimed not as a plain necessity but as an indispensible duty, points to a confusion of natural and positive law, similar to that manifested by Locke. It was only on the basis of such confusion that Locke could assert the right of the people to reclaim their original liberties for the choosing of a new legislature in the place of the one refusing to govern according to the popular will. Similarly it was only in consequence of such confusion that the French Constitution of 1793, failing to provide for any legal method of changing this Constitution, stated in Article 28 of the Declara-

[6] *Ibid.*, Articles 26-27, 29, 31.

[7] *Ibid.*, Article 35.

tion, as an article of national faith the political truism that: "A people has always the right to revise, reform and change its Constitution" and that "one generation cannot subject to its laws the generations of the future." [8]

The Constitution of 1793 was submitted to and approved by popular vote throughout France, but it was never put into effect. It represents the extreme expression of the theory of popular Sovereignty as visioned by the French people during the period of the revolution. The principle expressed in Article 28 has been liberally applied in French constitutional history, more so, in fact, than in the existence of any other nation. The proposed fundamental law of 1793 was replaced two years later by that of the year III (1795) of the Republic. Positing national rather than popular Sovereignty, the Constitution of 1795 closely resembled in this respect the first constitution of revolutionary France, i. e. that of 1791, inasmuch as it provided that: "Sovereignty resides essentially in the universality of the people," that "No individual, no partial gathering of citizens can assume sovereignty," and that "No one can, without legal delegation, exercise any authority, nor fill any public function." [9]

With the Constitution of the year VIII (1800) began a period of reaction leading to the return of the practical absolutism of the Napoleonic Empire to be followed by various stages of constitutional monarchism and republican rule, finally ending in the re-assertion of the principle of popular, or rather, national Sovereignty of the Third Republic.

[8] In this connection see Jefferson's idea of the compact, referred to above, note 3.

[9] Declaration, Articles 17-19.

CHAPTER IV

The Theories of Kant, Hegel and Fichte

Kant. The theories of State, Sovereignty and Law expressed by Kant were devoloped at a time when the ideas of the French Revolution were beginning to assert their influence in the rest of Europe for both good and evil. As an antidote to the prevailing doctrine of the Sovereignty of the monarch the doctrine of national or popular Sovereignty was laying the groundwork if not for the limitation, then at least for the definition in legal form, of the sovereign powers of kings and princes. On the other hand, in the abandonment of national in favor of popular Sovereignty, the revolutionary extremists had sowed the seed from which sprang the doctrine of the supremacy of the masses as distinguished from the citizenry forming the Nation, which doctrine in turn implied the destruction not only of monarchical rule, but of the existence of Nation and State. It was on the basis of this political background that Kant developed his theory of State, Sovereignty and Law, first published in 1796 as the Science of Right (or Law), to form the first part of his Metaphysics of Morals, the sequel and completion of the Foundation for a Metaphysics of Morals, published in 1785. [1]

Greatly attracted by Rousseau's political writings, Kant accepted the contract theory not as a historical reality but rather as a fiction which best served to explain the origin of the State. "It is not from any Experience prior to the appearance of an external authoritative Legislation, that we learn of the maxim of natural violence among men, and

[1] Kant, The Philosophy of Law....tr. from the German by W. Hastie.... 1887. Preface.

their evil tendency to engage in war with each other. Nor is it assumed here that it is merely some particular historical condition or fact, that makes public legislative constraint necessary; for however well-disposed or favourable to Right men may be considered to be of themselves, the rational Idea of a state of Society not yet regulated by Right, must be taken as our starting-point. This Idea implies that before a legal state of Society can be publicly established, individual Men, Nations and States can never be safe against violence from each other; and this is evident from the consideration that every one of his own Will naturally does *what seems good and right in his own eyes,* entirely independent of the opinion of others. Hence, unless the institution of Right is to be renounced, the first thing incumbent on men is to accept the Principle that it is necessary to leave the state of Nature, in which every one follows his own inclinations, and to form a union of all those who cannot avoid coming into reciprocal communication and thus subject themselves in common to the external restraint of public compulsory Laws.... Such is the primary Obligation, on the part of all men, to enter into the relations of a Civil State of Society." [2] Positing like Rousseau, the freedom of the individual in the hypothetical pre-civic state, Kant too attempted to preserve this freedom in the Society which has become a State. By the original contract people were supposed to have set aside their unregulated freedom of action only to receive back their liberty in a legal dependence in a juridical State.[3]

[2] *Ibid.*, pp. 163-164.

[3] "The act by which a people is represented as constituting itself into a State, is termed THE ORIGINAL CONTRACT. This is properly only an outward mode of representing the idea by which the rightfulness of the process of organizing the Constitution may be made conceivable. According to this representation, all and each of the people give up

Kant thus agrees with Rousseau in placing the supreme or sovereign power of the State in the legislature and in recognizing law as the supreme will of the State.[4] But he goes beyond Rousseau in the deductions drawn from this proposition. Law being the supreme will of the State, it must follow, so Kant holds, that law can do no wrong to the individual. It is so holy and inviolable that it is practically a crime even to cast doubt upon it, or to suspend its operation even for a moment. According to Kant "the origin of the Supreme Power is practically *inscrutable* by the People who are placed under its authority.... For as the People, in order to be able to adjudicate with a title of Right regarding the Supreme Power in the State, must be regarded as already united under one common legislative Will, it cannot judge otherwise than as the present Supreme Head of the State....wills." Kant considers futile the question "whether an actual contract of Subjection....originally preceded" the Civil Government as

their external Freedom in order to receive it immediately again as Members of a Commonwealth. The Commonwealth is the people viewed as united altogether into a State. And thus it is not to be said that the individual in the State has sacrificed *a part* of his inborn external Freedom for a particular purpose; but he has abandoned his wild lawless Freedom wholly, in order to find all his proper Freedom again entire and undiminished, but in the form of a regulated order of dependence, that is, in a Civil State regulated by laws of Right. This relation of Dependence thus arises out of his own regulative law-giving Will." (*Ibid.*, pp. 169-170).

[4] "The legislative power, viewed in its rational Principle, can only belong to the united Will of the People. For, as all Right ought to proceed from this Power, it is necessary that its Laws should be unable to do wrong to any one whatever. Now, if any *one* individual determines anything in the State in contradistinction to *another*, it is always possible that he may perpetrate a wrong on that other; but this is never possible when *all* determine and decree what is to be Law to themselves.... Hence it is only the united and consenting Will of all the People—in so far as Each of them determines the same thing about all, and all determine the same thing about each—that ought to have the power of enacting Law in the State." (*Ibid.*, p. 166).

a fact; or whether on the contrary, "the Power arose first and the Law only followed afterwards. . . ." But not only are these questions entirely aimless for the people who are now in submission to civil law, they are "even fraught with subtile danger to the State." So dangerous, in fact, are they that "should the Subject, after having dug down to the ultimate origin of the State, rise in opposition to the present ruling Authority, he would expose himself as a Citizen, according to the Law and with full Right, to be punished, destroyed, or outlawed." [5]

From the sanctity and divine origin of the law as the supreme will of the State expressed by the legislature it follows, according to Kant, that the supreme power in the State has only rights, and no compulsory duties to the subject. For according to Kant: "A law which is so holy and inviolable that it is *practically* a crime even to cast doubt upon it, or to suspend its operation even for a moment, is represented of itself as necessarily derived from some Supreme unblamable Lawgiver. And this is the meaning of the maxim. 'All Authority is from God'; which proposition does not express the *historical foundation* of the Civil Constitution, but an ideal Principle of the Practical Reason. It may be otherwise rendered thus, 'It is a Duty to obey the Law of the existing Legislative Power, be its origin what it may.' Hence it follows that the Supreme Power in the State has only Rights, and no (compulsory) Duties toward the Subject." [6]

But as the law is thus divine and the legislative power irreproachable, so is the executive power irresistible. The ideal executive is the king, who is in control of the enforcement of the law. Revolution naturally is held to be illegal,

[5] *Ibid.*, p. 174.
[6] *Ibid.*, pp. 174-175.

but when it comes, and a new Government is formed, obedience to the new authorities becomes as much of a duty as it was a crime to disobey the former.[7]

The significance of Kant's doctrine of the State, Sovereignty and Law is found: (1) in the great stress which he lays upon the sanctity and absolute binding character of law which finds its ultimate authority in God, the source of all law; (2) in asserting the irresistible character of the executive; (3) in the theory that the people by the fictitious act of the original contract have placed themselves in the position of subjectivity to the sovereign rulers of the State. In other words, that they can legitimately resist their rulers only through their representatives in the legislature, i. e., through the very Sovereign to whose law they owe absolute and abject obedience.

Hegel. As stated in Duguit's The Law and the State, Hegel's doctrine was first outlined in an article published in 1801 after the peace of Lunéville and entitled: Considerations sur l'état de l'Allemagne. The doctrine was tersely stated in the Encyclopädie der philosophischen Wissenschaften im Grundrisse, which appeared in 1817. It received development in full in the Grundlinien der Philosophie des Rechts oder Naturrecht und Staatswissenschaft, published in 1821 and constituting the eighth volume of Hegel's complete works published by his students from 1832-1887.[8]

During this period Hegel saw the French Revolution and its creation, the French Republic, give way to the nationalistic absolutism of the Empire of the First Napoleon. In Germany, on the other hand, he witnessed the collapse of the Holy Roman Empire of the German Nation

[7] *Ibid.*, p. 175 ff.

[8] Duguit, The Law and the State, p. 57, note 2.

and the destruction of Prussia at the hand of the French conqueror. It is true, he lived to see the establishment of the Confederation of the German States in 1815. But this Confederation was but a league of independent commonwealths, and as such a far cry from the expectation of those who had pinned their faith in the promises of the Holy Alliance for the creation of a National union of the German States in the form of a new German Empire.

It is not so strange then that according to the fundamental principles of Hegelian philosophy every idea implies its own negation. Being implies non-being. It is by a progressive conciliation of these conflicting ideas that we arrive, according to Hegel, at a final category constituting the unity of all contradictory concepts, i. e. the absolute idea. Applying these principles of being, non-being, and their conciliation in the concept of becoming to the theory of the State and Law, Hegel posits the individual as the fundamental idea whose negation is civic society conceived as inconsistent with the idea of the individual. The institution effecting the conciliation or synthesis of the contradictory ideas of individual and civic society is the State representing Society as a political as distinguished from a civic organization.

Hegel thus had no need in his system of State and Government for the original contract as the beginning of organized society. He held that from the concept of the original contract there result consequences which destroy the divine existing in itself, and its absolute authority and its majesty.[9] Hegel's conception of the basic elements of Society is one of solidarity or interdependence, or as defined by him, a system of individual and mutual needs and

[9] Hegel, Grundlinien der Philosophie des Rechts (Werke. Vollst. Ausg....1832-45, vol. viii, p. 312 ff).

their satisfaction.[10] To eliminate the danger attached to this condition and to assume the satisfaction of these social needs, Government is added and Society becomes the State. Government eliminates this risk by formulating the moral idea, or subjective right, into law and by enforcing what it has formulated. Thus Family, Society and State are progressive stages in the realization or externalization of the moral idea or of subjective right.[11]

Like Rousseau and Kant, Hegel attempts to preserve the liberty of the individual as a member of the State. But, he says: ". . . . For liberty we must not start from the individuality, nor from the consciousness, but only from the essence of consciousness, for whether man knows it or not, this essence is realized as an autonomous power, in which individuals are only moments. The State is the march of God in the world. Its foundation is the power of reason, realised as will. . . ." [12]

"The principle of the modern State has this extraordinary strength and depth that it allows the principle of subjectivity to complete itself to an extreme of personal particularity and yet, at the same time, brings back into it, substantial unity. . . . The characteristic idea of the State in the modern epoch is that the State is the realization of liberty, not according to subjective liking, but according to the notion of willing, that is to say its divinity."[13]

So far Hegel follows Kant in asserting the divine character of the State or the State's authority. But he goes

[10] *Ibid.*, Die bürgerliche Gesellschaft, p. 246 ff.

[11] *Ibid.*, Der Staat, p. 312 ff.

[12] *Ibid.*, p. 320.

[13] *Ibid.*, p. 322.

even further than Kant in extending this divine aspect to the authority or prerogative of the prince or monarch.

According to Hegel the concept of the Monarch represents one of the most difficult concepts within the sphere of rational reflection inasmuch as reflective reasoning does not proceed beyond isolated definition and therefore knows no more than causes, finite aspects and deduction from causes. "Thus it represents the dignity of the Monarch as something deducible not only in its formal aspect but also with regard to its purpose, while [in reality] the concept [of the dignity of the Monarch] signifies that it is not derivative but originating in itself (das schlechthin aus sich Anfangende)." And Hegel concludes, "the conception which most nearly approaches this realization is the one which represents the right of the Monarch as founded upon divine authority, because in such a notion is contained the unconditional aspect (das Unbedingte) of the Monarch's right." [14] Admitting that errors have grown out of this conception, he thinks that it is a problem for the philosopher to "determine that part which is truly divine in the Monarch. (Die Aufgabe der philosophischen Betrachtung ist es, eben dies Göttliche zu begreifen)." [15] This Sovereign, in part divine, is the synthesis of all the State's powers, he is the bearer of the omnipotence, and the Sovereignty of the State.

All three branches of the Government participate in the act of legislation. The Monarch as the holder of the sovereign power of the State must see to it that all laws find obedience. The Government in the form of councils of the Crown offers the superior knowledge needed for the proper legislation. Parliament cooperates by offering valuable in-

[14] *Ibid.*, pp. 366-367.

[15] *Ibid.*, p. 367.

formation and by giving publicity to matters exerts a certain control over the legislative activity of the other participants which tends towards the efficiency and usefulness of the law.[16]

Quite apparently under the influence of the doctrine of national Sovereignty of the French Revolution, Hegel distinguishes between the Sovereignty of the Monarch and that of the Nation. Positing the Sovereignty of the Monarch as shown above, he holds that the Sovereignty of the people manifests itself in the fact that the mass of individuals forming the Nation are actually organized as a politically independent State under a supreme Government or a sovereign Monarch. Thus he would concede Sovereignty to a State like Great Britain, while he would deny the same to the people of England or Scotland. In no other sense does he admit the Sovereignty of the people to exist. Referring to the conception of Sovereignty as the supremacy of the *demos* Hegel writes: "One can thus say also of Sovereignty within the State (nach Innen) that it resides in the people, if one generally speaks of the whole, in the sense that as shown above. . . . Sovereignty belongs to the State. But Sovereignty of the people in the sense in which one has begun to speak of it in modern times, i. e. Sovereignty of the people as distinguished from Sovereignty existing in the Monarch—belongs to the confused thoughts based upon the barren[17] concept (wüste Vorstellung) of the people. The people, taken without its Monarch and without the organization of the whole, which is the necessary and immediate consequence of it, is a shapeless mass, which is no longer a State, no longer hav-

[16] *Ibid.*, Die bürgerliche Gesellschaft, p. 270 ff.

[17] The translation of the adjective "wüste" as "lawlessness" as found in Duguit's The Law and the State (p. 92) goes too far inasmuch as lawlessness suggests more than the mere absense of a legal order.

ing such decision as can be found only in the organized whole in itself, that is to say, in Sovereignty, in Government, in tribunals, in a supreme council, in States. It is only when these elements are related to the organization, to the life of the State appearing in the people, that what is called in a general way, the people, ceases to be an indeterminate abstraction."[18] It is this clear cut distinction between Sovereignty of the people conceived as the Sovereignty of the Nation organized as an independent State, and the supremacy of the masses viewed as an unorganized, non-political multitude of individuals, which constitutes Hegel's vital contribution to the slowly developing outlines of the modern conception of the State.

Fichte. Beginning his philosophical career under Kant's concept of the supremacy of the moral law and the inherent moral worth of man, Fichte conceived the twofold plan of presenting to his fellowmen in a more easily understandable form the moral philosophy of Kant and the basic principles of political liberalism underlying the apparent excesses of the French Revolution. In 1793 he published his first attempts in this direction, the one entitled: Demand for the Return by the Princes of Europe of the Freedom of Thought,[19] and the other called: Contributions for the Correction of the Popular Judgment of the French Revolution.[20] It was in the Beiträge (Contributions) that Fichte sought to explain the fundamental ideas of liberty, liberal government and the need for progressive reform in the organization of the State. These first attempts were followed in 1798 by the Foundations of Natural Law,[21]

[18] Grundlinien der Philosophie des Rechts, pp. 367-368.

[19] Zurückforderung der Denkfreiheit von den Fürsten Europens.... (Sämmtliche Werke, vol vi).

[20] Beiträge zur Berichtigung der Urtheile des Publicums über die französiche Revolution (Sämmtl. Werke, vol. vi).

[21] Grundlage des Naturrechts (Sämmtl. Werke, vol. iii).

containing Fichte's earlier conception of State and Government, and by the System of Morals [22] published in the same year. In 1810 appeared the Exclusive or Isolated Commercial State,[23] in which the author applied the liberal principles of the French Revolution in the sphere of public economics, advocating organized protection on the basis of an extremely socialistic organization of industry, commerce and trade. In 1806 the defeat of Prussia forced him to leave Berlin and to take refuge successively in Pomerania, East Prussia and Denmark. After his return to Berlin in 1807 he delivered his famous Addresses to the German Nation,[24] in which patriotism rivalled with pure reason in the effort to arouse the German people to a new consciousness of national ideals and greatness. Fichte's last work, the System of the State, published posthumously in 1820,[25] contained his later Utopian idea of the State and Society, based on the principles of pure reason. Fichte died in January 1814, in the midst of Germany's struggle for national liberty and regeneration.

Starting from the assumption that consciousness of the existence of the rational and practical self implies consciousness of other selves, and that the existence of the ego thus leads to the admission of the existence of other egos,[26] Fichte holds that this mutual consciousness is the basis of law (Recht), or as Dunning renders the term

[22] Das System der Sittenlehre (Sämmtl. Werke, vol. iv).

[23] Der Geschlossene Handelsstaat. (Sämmtl. Werke, vol. iii).

[24] Reden an die deutsche Nation (Sämmtl. Werke, vol. vii).

[25] Die Staatslehre (Sämmtl. Werke, vol. iv).

[26] Grundlage des Naturrechts. Erstes Hauptstück. Zweiter Lehrsatz: "Man, as all finite beings in general, becomes man only among men; and since he can be nothing but man, and would be nothing if not man—there must be several (mehrere) men, if there are any men at all" (p. 39).

Recht in this connection, the basis of social regulation.[27] Denying the existence of natural *rights* in man's natural condition he claims that there was originally only natural *right*. This he defines as "the absolute right of the person to exist in the world of sense only as cause and never as effect." [28] However, for man to be a cause in the world of sense means to have a will, and the problem of the State is that of evolving in the world of sense through the Staatsbürgervertrag a will "in which private will and general will are synthetically united." [29] This problem of uniting private and general will Fichte tried to solve by a threefold contract, first: the property contract (Eigenthumsvertrag), by which each individual agrees with each other individual to relinquish any claim to the other's property and by which each recognizes the extent of the other's property; second: the protection contract (Schutzvertrag), by which each pledges the other his share of protectionist force for the maintenance of the property agreement; and third: the union contract (Vereinigungsvertrag), by which each unites with each for the effectuation of the objects of the preceding contracts. It is the last one of these contracts, completing the Staatsbürgervertrag, by which, according to Fichte, the sovereign State, man's natural condition, is established. As the individual thus by the Vereinigungsvertrag becomes part of the whole State and as the whole State becomes the sovereign and judge of the individual, Fichte speaks of a fourth con-

[27] *Ibid.*, Dritter Lehrsatz: "The finite rational being cannot posit other finite rational beings outside of himself, except by positing himself as existing in a certain relation which is called the relation of law." (p. 41).

[28] *Ibid.*, Erstes Capitel. Die Rechtslehre. Deduction des Urrechts, p. 111 ff.

[29] *Ibid.*, Zweiter Theil. Vom Staatsbürgervertrage, p. 191 ff.

tract, the Unterwerfungsvertrag (submission or subjection contract) which, he adds, is, however, only hypothetical.[30]

In his earlier writings Fichte held that the individual did not become merged in the State but gave up no more than was actually essential for the State to function. As he did not recognize a state of nature as the pre-civic condition of man, nor the original possession of natural rights, Fichte's doctrine had no room for the theory of the transfer of the Sovereignty of the people to the State. All that the individual yielded was a claim for the other man's property, which latter he defines as "rights of free action in the world of sense," [31] and this claim he yielded not to the State but to the other man. To the State he transferred his share of the obligation to enforce the conditions of the property and protection agreements. In his later period, however, Fichte approached the position of Hegel, holding it to be the function of the State to give to each for the first time his own, to install him for the first time in his property, and then first to protect him in it.[32]

Fichte's importance for German constitutional development and for constitutional development in general was found in his application of these principles to the actual system of government of the State thus created. The individual will united with the general will of the people was expressed as the sovereign will of the State by the laws passed by the legislature. The functions of the Government, i. e. of the executive, including the judiciary, can be exercised only by persons or organs representative of the people. As well summarized by Dunning: "The government might be either monarchic, or aristocratic, hereditary or elective, it could never be democratic, that

[30] *Ibid.*, p. 206.

[31] *Ibid.*, p. 195.

[32] Der geschlossene Handelsstaat, book 1, chapter 1.

is, the people as a whole could not act as administration. To insure that the sovereign will of the people, as embodied in the laws (Gesetze) forming the constitution, should not be overridden by the government, Fichte conceived an institution named the ephorate that he regarded as indispensable to a rational constitution (vernunft- und rechtmässige Staatsverfassung). The right of final judgment upon the conduct of the government must inhere necessarily in the people as a whole. To assign to any organ of the government the function of deciding whether the laws were being properly administered, would be to make that organ supreme; to assign to any organ even the function of deciding when the people should be called upon to express their opinion upon the situation, would have the same tendency of exalting the government over the sovereign. Hence the need for a body of ephors, wholly distinct from the government, and having no other duties than that of setting in motion, at the time they judged proper, the machinery through which the will of the sovereign people as to the constitution and laws can be expressed." [33]

Fichte thus clearly conceived the Government as distinct from the State and as the State's functionaries and agents. Defining the constitution as the expression of the sovereign will of the people by which the branches of government are legally bound, he failed to realize, however, that this legal dependency was no more effective in controlling the extra-governmental body of the ephors than in assuring the constitutionality of the actions of the Government. This failure Fichte realized in his later years. Still, as Dunning remarks, he found nothing to suggest in the place of the ephorate, "but the purely ideal conception that the functions of government should be

[33] Dunning, A History of Political Theories from Rousseau to Spencer, pp. 146-147.

entrusted only to all-wise philosophers, whose pure and unerring intelligence would never deviate from the straight line."[34]

The Eclectic Aspect of these Theories. What has been said above of the opportunist aspect of the doctrines of Hooker, Hobbes, Locke and Rousseau, applies with equal justice to the political and juristic theories of Kant, Hegel and Fichte. The decades in which Kant, Hegel and Fichte evolved their systems represent a period of national and social demoralization in the German States such as had not been witnessed since the fall of the Roman and Byzantine Empires. It was the utter disappearance of a national morale and authority which evoked the absolutist tendencies in the doctrines of Kant and Hegel. On the other hand, the hopes of a political and social enfranchisement raised by the French Revolution, had been almost completely frustrated by the united efforts of the German dynasties fearing for their own existence. It was the reaction to this failure which called forth the liberal and to some extent radical notes in the theories of Fichte.

But aside from this apparent opportunist attitude of Kant, Hegel and Fichte, one cannot escape the realization of the strongly eclectic character of their political doctrines. Thus we find Bodin's idea of the legal and moral absolutism of the prince recurring in the Kantian theory of the sanctity and irresistibility of the law and Rousseau's concept of the supremacy of the general will as Kant's theory of the sovereign character of the legislature. In Hegel's idealization of the State we recognize the principle, exaggerated though it is, of national Sovereignty as expressed in the first constitution of revolutionary France, while his partial deification of the monarch cannot but remind us of Bodin's endeavors in the same direction. At the same time we discover in Hegel's doc-

[34] *Ibid.*, p. 147.

trine an appreciable recognition of the reformatory social tendencies of the French Revolution, manifesting itself in his conception of solidarity and interdependence as the basic element of society. Fichte's system consisting chiefly in elaboration of the liberalizing doctrines of the French Revolution as applied to the practical questions of national life and government contains a strange admixture of rationalized despotism as for instance in his conception of the extra-constitutional controlling functions of the ephorate or body of all-wise philosophers as the final arbiters of nation and governors.

Abstracting from their respective systems the outstanding and lasting elements we should say that Kant has given us the concept of the sanctity and finality of the law, Hegel the idea of the supremacy of the State, and Fichte the notion of the constitutional control of the governing magistracy. Stripped of the fanciful and Utopian dressing which these principles have received at the hands of their sponsors, they may be stated in logical or systematic order as follows: Sovereignty of the State conceived as the citizenry of the nation including its rulers; the supremacy of the law as the will of the State expressed by the legislature; definition, in the form of a fundamental law, of the prerogatives or functions of the various organs of the State, including those of the monarch himself, and finally, control of the actions of these organs in accordance with a definite legally or otherwise binding system. As thus stated these principles constitute the foundation upon which the modern conception of the Rechtsstaat is based.[35]

[35] The term Rechtsstaat is not identical with the concept of the State as a juristic personality. It merely connotes the idea of a State in which government is carried on in accordance with more or less definitely established legal norms, rather than by the actions of personal rulers according to their own discretion or notion of what is best for their subjects. The idea of the Rechtsstaat may thus probably best be expressed by the term constitutional State as its nearest equivalent.

CHAPTER V.

THE AUSTINIAN OR ANALYTICAL SCHOOL

Austin's Theory of Law and Sovereignty. Austin's analytical treatment of Law and Sovereignty constitutes, like that of Bodin, an attempt to devise a theory of the State and its aspects by an analytical examination of the body politic as it is. In this attempt Austin, no more than Bodin, escaped the error of confounding the State as the political organization under which he lived and the State as an idea or type.

Defining law as a species of command, and positive law as a species of command emanating from a determined political superior, Austin posits this superior as the Sovereign of the independent political society.[1] The Sovereign thus defined is personal, "One or Number."

This Sovereign Austin places in contradistinction to the rest of the political society when he speaks of subjection as the correlative of Sovereignty. According to Austin, the mutual relation which subsists between that superior and the rest of the body politic "may be styled the relation of sovereign and subject, or the relation of sovereignty and subjection."[2]

[1] Austin, The Austinian Theory of Law....by W. Jethro Brown, London, 1906. pp. 4, 40, 41, 60.

[2] "....In order to an explanation of the marks which distinguish positive laws, I shall analyse the expression *sovereignty*, the correlative expression *subjection*, and the inseparably connected expression independent political society. For the essential difference of a positive law....may be stated thus. Every positive law, or every law simply and strictly so-called, is set by a sovereign person, or a sovereign body of persons, to a member or members of the independent polit-

In his attempt "to further elucidate the nature or essence of sovereignty, and of the independent political society which sovereignty implies" Austin calls attention to the following subjects or topics: "(1) The various shapes which sovereignty may assume, or the various possible forms of supreme government. (2) The real and imaginary limits which bound the power of sovereigns, and by which the power of sovereigns is supposed to be bounded. (3) The origin of government, with the origin of political society: or the causes of the habitual obedience which is rendered by the bulk of subjects, and from which the power of sovereigns to compel and restrain the refractory is entirely and mainly derived." [3]

The apparently synonymous use of the expressions "various shapes which sovereignty may assume or the various possible forms of supreme government" suggests that to Austin forms of Sovereignty and forms of Government are one and the same, or that Austin posits the Government as the Sovereign.[4]

ical society wherein that person or body is sovereign or supreme. Or (changing the expression) it is set by a monarch, or sovereign number, to a person or persons in a state of subjection to its author...." (*Ibid.*, p. 96).

"To that determinate superior, the other members of the society are subject: or on that determinate superior, the other members of the society are dependent. The position of its other members toward that determinate superior is *a state of subjection*, or a state of dependence. The mutual relation which subsists between that superior and them, may be styled *the relation of sovereign* and subject, or *the relation of* sovereignty and subjection" (*Ibid.*, p. 97).

[3] *Ibid.*, p. 117.

[4] This suggestion in fact is found to be expressly stated in the following where Austin asserts that: "An independent political society is divisible into two portions: namely, the portion of its members which is sovereign or supreme, and the portion of its members which is merely subject. The sovereignty can hardly reside in *all* the members of a society: for it can hardly happen that some of those mem-

The idea of Sovereignty as found in the constitutions of revolutionary France was clearly one of the supreme power residing in the whole body of the people forming the body politic, the governors and the governing included. By this sovereign body of the politically organized Nation the exercise of this Sovereignty was conceived as delegated to certain bodies which form the Government acting as the Nation's agents. Exercising Sovereignty under the French system was not possessing Sovereignty but acting in the name of the Sovereign in a capacity which commanded obedience only so long as the actions of the agents were in accordance with the terms of the commission or delegation. Government was the form or mode in which Sovereignty was exercised, it was not Sovereignty. In the French conception Sovereignty was the result of the consciousness of the desire to belong to the French body politic and of the realization of a system of control giving security and permanency to the fulfillment of this desire. Hence the French theory of Sovereignty did not bother itself about the fitness of each and every individual to possess and to exercise his share of Sovereignty. Austin, however, identifying Government, i. e. the exercise of Sovereignty, with its possession, of necessity fell into the vicious circle of concluding from these premises that not *all* can be in the possession of Sovereignty, because not *all* are fit to govern, i. e. to exercise Sovereignty. In Austin's

bers shall not be naturally incompetent to exercise sovereign powers. In most actual societies, the sovereign powers are engrossed by a single member of the whole, or are shared exclusively by a very few of its members and even in the actual societies whose government are esteemed popular, the sovereign number is a slender portion of the entire political community. An independent political society governed by itself, or governed by a sovereign body consisting of the whole community, is not impossible; but the existence of such societies is so extremely improbable, that, with this passing notice, I throw them out of my account" (*Ibid.*, p. 117).

conception Sovereignty is the action of governing, hence since not everybody is capable of governing, not everybody is capable of possessing Sovereignty. Thus, speaking of the governing body, one or number, Austin holds that: "......In case that sovereign portion consists of a single member, the supreme government is properly a *monarchy,* or the sovereign is properly a *monarch.* In case that sovereign portion consists of a number of members, the supreme government may be styled an aristocracy (in the generic meaning of the expression)." [5]

Austin was convinced that the system of Sovereignty and its location, which he described fitted the political system under which he lived and of which he was a subject member. According to Austin the determinate body which is sovereign in Great Britain is the British Parliament or the King in Parliament.[6] Though a monarch, the English King is not the Sovereign but only "a limb of the

[5] *Ibid.*, p. 118.

[6] "It comprises the only person who answers for the time being to the generic description of King. It comprises every person belonging to the class of peers who are entitled for the time being to vote in the upper house. It comprises every person belonging to the class of commoners who for the time being represent the commoners in Parliament. And, though every member of the British Parliament is of necessity determined by a specific or appropriate character, he is not a member of the parliament by reason of his bearing that character but by reason of his answering to the given generic description. It is not as being the individual George, but as being the individual who answers to the generic description of King, that George is King of Britain and Ireland, and a limb of the determined body which is sovereign or supreme therein. It is not as the individual Grey, or as being the individual Peel, that Grey is a member of the upper house, or Peel a member of the lower. Grey is a member of the upper house, as belonging to the class of peers entitled to vote therein. Peel is a member of the lower house, as answering the generic description representative of the Commons in Parliament." (*Ibid.*, pp. 56-57).

determinate body which is sovereign or supreme." [7] The other limbs are the body of peers and the members of the House of Commons. All three together form the determinate body which is the Sovereign. But while the King and the peers exercise their share of Sovereignty directly, the members of the House of Commons exercise their share of Sovereignty only as the representatives of the great body of the Commoners.[8]

Austin's theory of Sovereignty and its location is a compromise between Bodin's conception of Sovereignty as vested in the ruler, preferably the king, and the French theory of popular Sovereignty as residing in the Nation or the people. This compromise was dictated by the desire or necessity of evolving a system which would, at the same time, give due consideration to the prerogatives of the Crown and acknowledge and sanction the rights acquired by the English Commons. A king, to be a king, is still considered by Austin as possessing Sovereignty, even if it is only a part of the Sovereignty of the political society concerned. The same may be said of the peers, although it is not clear whether the peers are supposed to possess Sovereignty on the same basis upon which the king is vested with it, namely as co-rulers, or on the ground of the more modern principle of popular Sovereignty as representatives of the class from which they are appointed by the king. The recognition of the great body of Commons as one limb of the sovereign body in the British system of State was clearly unavoidable from the point of view of practical politics and historical realities.

It is through the different degrees and modes of such sharing of the supreme or sovereign power and by the method of identifying the possession of Sovereignty with

[7] *Ibid.*, p. 56.

[8] *Ibid.*, pp. 56, 58.

the action of governing that Austin explains what he calls the different forms of government. In the same way he attempts to make applicable to other State systems a theory of Sovereignty and of its location, for which in reality he can claim by rights no more than that it may fit the British system and others like it.

Brown's and Dicey's Modification of Austin's Theory. Later English authorities, seeing that Austin's theory could not be universally applied to other State systems, have gone to considerable lengths in modifying this theory in order to make it at least more generally applicable. It is in consequence of these attempts that we come finally to the recognition of the juristic conception of the State and Sovereignty as the only system which seems to apply to every State, i. e. every sovereign State, no matter what its actual form of government may be.

Brown, for instance, holds that the concept of Sovereignty must of necessity differ when considered by different departments of human thought. Thus the student of international law considers Sovereignty in the relation of State to State, or as Austin would say, as independence; the lawyer as supremacy recognized by law; the political philosopher as political Sovereignty or practical supremacy in the internal affairs of the State.[9] Considering Sovereignty from the point of view of political science Brown states that political Sovereignty is practical supremacy. "But where in the modern state like our own," he asks, "is this supremacy to be found?"[10] Without going

[9] *Ibid.*

[10] Brown seems to hold that a generally applicable theory of Sovereignty cannot be found. "Sovereignty, being an attribute of human association, must be subject like human association to the laws of development. Generally describable as some kind of power or authority in some kind of political community, sovereignty must necessarily

beyond the British Constitution, he finds it possible to place this political Sovereignty in at least four different bodies: (1) The dominating power in the government. (2) The electoral body. (3) The popular majority. (4) The State as a moral organism.[11] The first three of these catagories consist of different groups of members of the body politic, the fourth is the body politic itself.

Speaking of this definition of Sovereignty and its location as applicable to other State systems Brown is of the opinion that "If we were to extend our analysis to other states, some of the above expressions must be made more general, some new types must be added. For present purposes," he thinks "the list may be accepted as it stands. Each of the types to which reference is made has some claim to answer to the description of the political sovereign which has been suggested by Dicey. 'That body is politically sovereign the will of which is ultimately obeyed

change as communities grow. Any account of it which affects to be universal is almost certain to be misleading. Failure to recognize this simple fact, attempts to find universal theories when provisional theories alone can be at once possible and useful, have resulted in a fatal divorce between doctrine and reality" (p. 273). However, Brown's apprehensions in this respect seem to be due to Austin's, Dicey's and his own failure to divorce the idea of possession or location from the exercise of Sovereignty, which in turn is the result of their error of identifying location and possession of Sovereignty with the function of governing, i. e. acting in the name of and for the Sovereign. This phase of the question will be discussed in more detail in connection with the juristic theory of State and Sovereignty.

[11] "If we are disposed towards the legal view of things, we may say that in Great Britain the House of Commons is the political sovereign; or, if we are somewhat less legally minded, we may say that the real supremacy does not rest with the House of Commons, but with the electors of the United Kingdom; or again, shaking off the fetters of legalism altogether, we may say that the whole community is sovereign, meaning by the community either a sum of individuals or an organic unity. Thus, without going beyond the British Constitution, we find at least four distinct types of conception of sovereignty for the

by the citizens of the State'."[12] He continues to explain that "the choice between the four types mentioned must depend upon conditions of time and circumstance," since, "the theory of sovereignty must keep pace with the progress of society" as illustrated by "territorial expansion, the extension of political power to new classes of the community, and the increase in the strength of the various bonds, material, intellectual and moral, which unite the citizens to one another and to the State." As stated by Professor Brown "the end of the first phase is the large political aggregate; the end of the second, the democratic community; the end of the third, the realization of a national life" and, "as progress in one or other of these phases absorbs the energies of the State, the seat of sovereignty is changed."[13]

Realizing that the British Parliament, though formally the supreme legisaltive body of the British body politic, is in reality nevertheless in a certain state of dependence on the will of the British electorate, Austin had tried to meet this fact by the device of the delegation of Sovereignty from the electorate to the House of Commons as the body possessing and exercising the share of Sovereignty thus delegated by the electors. Brown holds that in doing this Austin confused political and legal Sovereignty.

As we have seen, Brown differentiates between political and legal Sovereignty as two different aspects of supreme power considered from two different departments of

purpose of political science. These types may be expressed briefly as follows: (1) The dominating power in the government. (2) The electoral body. (3) The popular majority. (4) The State as a moral organism." (*Ibid.*, pp. 276-277).

[12] *Ibid.*, p. 277.

[13] *Ibid.*, pp. 277-278.

thought, namely that of political theory or philosophy and that of jurisprudence. Dicey, on the other hand, posits political and legal Sovereignty as two parallel forces or powers within the political unit. He writes:

"Sovereignty, like many of Austin's conceptions, is a generalization drawn in the main from English law...... In England we are accustomed to the existence of a supreme legislative body, i. e. a body which can make or unmake every law; and which, therefore, cannot be bound by any law. This is, from a legal point of view, the true conception of a sovereign........

"........If the term 'sovereignty' be thus used, the sovereign power under the English Constitution is clearly 'Parliament.' But the word 'sovereignty' is sometimes employed in a political rather than in a strictly legal sense. That body is 'politically' sovereign or supreme in a state, the will of which is ultimately obeyed by the citizens of the state. In this sense of the word the electors of Great Britain may be said to be, together with the Crown and the Lords, or perhaps, in strict accuracy, independently of the King and the peers, the body in which sovereignty is vested......... But this is a political, not a legal fact. The electors can in the long run always enforce their will. But the courts will take no notice of the will of the electors. The judges know nothing about any will of the electors of the people except in so far as that will is expressed by an Act of Parliament, and would never suffer validity of a statute to be questioned on the ground of its having been passed or being kept alive in opposition to the wishes of the electors. The political sense of the word 'sovereignty' is, it is true, fully as important as the legal sense or more so. But the two significations, though intimately connected together, are essentially different, and in some part of his work, Austin has apparently confused the one sense with the other." [14]

Modern Trend towards the Juristic Conception of the State. Considering legal Sovereignty, i. e. Sovereignty in the domain of jurisprudence, Brown defines this "Sovereignty without qualifying epithet" as "supremacy recognized by law." [15] He holds that "the location of this supremacy like the location of political sovereignty, has varied from time to time." As to the location of this Sovereignty in recent times Brown expresses himself in part as follows: "The *possibility* of the location of the sovereignty in the State itself is implicitly recognized in all modern theories which state legal limitations upon the power which ranks highest in the hierarchy of State institutions. The sovereign is the source of all law, and so cannot be limited by law; where a legal limitation is held to exist upon a power claiming to be sovereign, we are compelled to infer that legal theory looks beyond the pretended sovereign to the State itself as true sovereign and ultimate source of law........

".......When once the conclusion has been reached that under conceivable conditions sovereignty may reside in the State itself, the more startling conclusion is suggested that sooner or later the location of sovereignty in the State must be accepted as an axiom by legal theory in all highly developed communities. Even where legal absolutism can be attributed to some definite legislative institution, sooner or later the question is certain to arise whether, after all, formal supremacy can be attributed to that institution save as an organ of the State. In a multitude of ways the State, as owner of its territory, as in-

[14] Dicey, Law of the Constitution, 8. ed., pp. 71-72.

[15] Brown in his edition of Austin, p. 281.

vested with property and the dubious blessing of a National Debt, demands legal recognition. But if once the law recognizes the State as an entity capable of rights and duties, it is almost compelled to attribute sovereignty to that entity, and to regard the supreme law-making institution as merely an actualization of a formal supremacy which in the last analysis can only be found in the State itself." [16]

The acceptance of legal Sovereignty as here defined and its application to the British body politic would divest the British king of his share of Sovereginty as a possession. He would under this theory, together with the House of Peers and the House of Commons not possess, but exercise Sovereignty as the representative of the real Sovereign, the State. The same would of course hold true *mutatis mutandis,* for the House of Peers and the great body of the British electorate or their representatives in the House of Commons. While admitting this to be the logical conclusion to reach, Brown is apparently not yet ready to go to such extremes for England. To him the conception of political Sovereignty still appears to be the necessary means of explaining those activities of the State or of the organs of government, which under a different system, may be looked upon as nothing more than acts performed in the exercise of Sovereignty in accordance with implied or expressed conditions of delegation. Thus he holds that in jurisprudence the conception of Sovereignty may refer to the formal supremacy of "(1) A government; (2) The highest law-making body, ordinary or extraordinary; (3) The State as a juristic person." [17]

[16] *Ibid.*, p. 284.
[17] *Ibid.*, pp. 285-286.

Considered historically or rather retrospectively Brown's position is not an unnatural one to take in the case of England where the transformation from kingship by divine right to a monarch whose royal prerogatives are largely curtailed, and the present position of supremacy of the Commons have been achieved by political action. The situation is quite different in a country like the United States where the foundation of the State coincided or was immediately followed by the formulation of the Constitution and where, at least in theory, all future political action was supposed to be carried out in accordance with the Constitution as the fundamental and supreme law of the land. Of this society it can be said that, at the time when its political organization was effected, there were present in the group certain general common interests. These interests were definitely expressed in the Declaration of Independence and in the Constitution itself. The formulation of the Constitution showed the existence of a general desire for an effective system of control by the group over the individual. The acceptance of the Constitution guaranteed the realization of this desire and the formation of a machinery of government in accordance with the fundamental law of the group and for the purpose of maintaining and carrying out this law. Of this body politic it can be said that it started its career by positing law as the essence of its authority over its members and as the guiding norm for the mode of appointment of its governing agents and for their activities in exercising control in the name of the group. It is to this body politic that there may be applied, without difficulty, and from its very beginning, the juristic conception of the State, which conceives the State as Society politically organized and Sovereignty as the "supreme legally legitimizing will" of the State.

But the analytical jurist positing the juristic character of the State and Sovereignty is not concerned with the historical beginnings of existing States, nor with the origin of the State as a general concept. He is interested in the task of abstracting from the essential phenomena of States as they are, a formal concept applicable to the actualities of political reality and legal practice. Though Brown seems to insist upon viewing the problem retrospectively at least as far as England is concerned, he nevertheless admits that generally speaking not only legal, but also political supremacy, i. e. Sovereignty, is more and more being considered as residing in the nation as a political unit rather than in any one organ or body as a part of that unit. With regard to his statement concerning the probability of the general acceptance of the juristic theory of the State he maintains that it "has been reached by reference to formal conclusion," but he admits that "a similar conclusion is also suggested by considerations which go to the roots of things." [18] The meaning of this last phrase is revealed in the following significant admission. "As in the sphere of politics," he writes, "in proportion as nations have come to self-consciousness, political sovereignty or practical supremacy is seen to reside in the community regarded as an organic totality, so also in the sphere of Jurisprudence, those who seek to think things together, to bring legal formulae into some relation with the actual tendencies of social life, are impelled to look beyond the sovereignty of Court etiquette, and beyond the sovereignty of parliamentary institutions and constitution-revising assemblies, to the totality of the community which King, Parliament or Assembly but represent. But while in politics men have sought to give expression to thoughts and ideas that were clamouring for recognition

[18] *Ibid.*, pp. 284-285.

in some theory of Society as a moral organism, the tendency in Jurisprudence has been rather to make use of a conception which existed in germ in Roman law and was suggested by the attempts of lawyers to find some expression for the phenomena of group life as exhibited in the *universitas personarum*—the conception of a juristic person. The recognition and development of this conception represents the most important contribution to Jurisprudence which has been made in recent times." [19]

[19] *Ibid.*, p. 285.

CHAPTER VI.

Willoughby's Juristic Conception of the State

The Formal Aspect of the Theory. The essence of the juristic conception of the State and Sovereignty cannot be given more effectively than in the words of Professor Willoughby, its most authoritative exponent in the English speaking world.[1] Liberal recourse to Willoughby's own method of stating his case seems justified also in view of the criticism and the attempted modification of the theory to be considered below.

To begin with, the juristic conception of the State is not concerned with the antecedents or even the origin of the State. Accepting the State as being in existence and its political institutions as it finds them, the analytical school of jurisprudence views both the State and its organization from the purely legal aspect. "It does not inquire into the ethical right of the State to exist, nor as to its ethically legitimate sphere of authority........ It is indifferent to all questions as to the relative merits of different forms of government."[2] On the contrary "it takes political institutions as it finds them.......it views them in a single aspect, namely, as legal institutions, and

[1] Professor Willoughby's theory was first presented in his book, An Examination of the Nature of the State, 1896, re-issued in 1911. A concise and short statement of it is found in his article The Juristic Conception of the State (The American Political Science Review, vol. xii, 1918, pp. 192-208). The theory has been fully elaborated in his recent work: The Fundamental Concepts of Public Law, 1924. Quotations given in the present study, unless otherwise stated, are from the article cited, i. e. The Juristic Conception of the State.

[2] p. 193.

as thus viewed, seeks to ascertain the essential qualities exhibited by them." [3]

The State, so Willoughby concedes, may of course be regarded from a number of standpoints. "It may be studied sociologically as one of the factors as well as one of the results of communal life; it may be examined historically for the purpose of ascertaining the part which it has played in the life of humanity, its varying phases of development being traced and their several causes and results determined; it may be considered as an entity, to the existence and activities of which are applied the ethical criteria which the moralist and philosopher establish; it may be psychologically surveyed in order to make plain the manifestations of will, emotion and judgment which support and characterize its life; it may be regarded from the purely practical standpoint to determine how it may be most efficiently organized and operated; and, finally, it may be envisaged and studied simply as an instrumentality for the creation and enforcement of laws." But, "it is with the state as viewed in the last aspect, that analytical political philosophy is concerned." [4]

Before we can enter into the consideration of the essentials of the State thus viewed from the purely legal aspect, reference must be made to Willoughby's warning "that analytical political theory is a purely formalistic inquiry" and that it is not the task of the political analytical philosopher "to seek substantive truth." [5] As stated by the author: "The point of departure of the analytical jurist is that in all communities which have reached any degree of definite political organization, public affairs, whether

[3] pp. 193-194.
[4] p. 192.
[5] p. 193.

domestic or international, are not carried on in a haphazard manner, without system or fixed principles, but are governed by bodies of rules logically related to one another and all depending, as deductive conclusions, upon certain assumptions regarding the juristic nature of the state, of its sovereignty, of its law, and of the relations which it bears towards other bodies politic as similarly viewed. Thus analytical political philosophy starts with certain primary assumptions or definitions from which, by deductive reasoning, it determines those principles which give a systematic and logical character to constitutional and international jurisprudence."[6]

The State and Sovereignty. With regard to the essentials of the doctrine of the juristic conception of the State as evolved by this purely formalistic inquiry we shall let Willoughby speak for himself, attempting to the best of our judgment to select only such passages as seem indispensable both for the presentation of the vital points and of the doctrine as a whole. Thus Willoughby states in part:

"The point from which the analytical political philosopher starts is that a politically organized group of individuals may be conceived of as constituting an essential unity, and that the entity thus created may be regarded as a person in the legal sense of the word; that is, as a being, existing in idea, possessing legal rights and obligations as distinguished from those of the individuals who, concretely viewed, make up its body politic, and that, as such a personality, it is, through organs of its own creation, capable of formulating and uttering a legal will with reference to matters within the jurisdiction conceded to it.

[6] pp. 193-194.

"Regarded as a legal person the prime characteristic of the state is that there is posited of it a will that is legally supreme. By its express command, or by its tacit acquiescence, it is thus viewed as the ultimate source of legality for every act committed by its own agents or by any persons whomsoever over whom it claims authority. This supreme legally legitimising will is termed sovereignty. The idea connoted by it is one purely of legal competence or jurisdiction. No element of actual power, (as distinguished from will), or of moral right, or of political expediency, is involved." [7]

"This unlimited legal competence which is predicated of the sovereign state connotes the authority to determine the legal rights and duties which shall exist so far as it is itself concerned, and to fix the territorial limits within which it will not permit, without its consent, the enforcement of other legal rights and duties which owe their existence to another sovereignty. This postulated legal omnipotence also carries with it the authority to declare, without reference to territorial limits, what persons shall be deemed to owe an allegiance to the state in question and an obedience to the commands which it utters. It thus results that areas of land and water, and all persons, whatever their other political relations and affiliations, are potentially subject to the legal control of any given state. That is, it is possible by a mere exercise of its sovereign will to bring them within a control, the legal validity of which its own courts cannot question." [8]

Willoughby does, of course, realize that under such an extension of the sovereign power of the individual State, controversies may arise "by reason of two or more states

[7] p. 194.
[8] p. 195.

claiming exclusive legal control over particular persons or particular pieces of land or sea." He considers that the adjustment and prevention of these conflicts is the task of international law and as such not subject to discussion in this connection. Nor does "the fact that the necessities of international life compel every sovereign state to refrain from the exercise, in certain respects, of a jurisdiction over persons and territory which it might, if it saw fit, bring within the scope of its legal will, ... in any wise or any degree, derogate from that legal omnipotency which, from a constitutional point of view, the sovereign state possesses. . . . . ." In substantiation of this conception of the Sovereignty of the State Willoughby refers to the fact that "the courts of all states uniformly hold themselves conclusively bound by the assertions of what is called the political departments of the government, of a claim of sovereignty whether with reference to a control of individuals or of territory."[9]

The Exercise of Sovereignty. So much for the sphere or extension of the State's legal omnipotence. Proceeding to the definition of Sovereignty from the point of view of its mode of exercise or manifestation Willoughby states in part as follows:

"Viewed as a quality or faculty of statehood, and as connoting legal omnipotence rather than physical power, sovereignty is, by its very nature, a unity. It is the name

[9] pp. 195-196. "The fact that the sovereignty of a state is not limited in its operation or exercise to a definite territory is shown by the circumstance that every state exercises a certain amount of legal authority, irrespective of locality. Thus, of course, all states exercise authority over the high seas. Again the subject of a state remains a subject, wherever he may happen to be, and is entitled to his state's protection as such and, furthermore, he may be held legally responsible to his state for what he does while in a foreign country. . . ." (*Ibid.*, p. 196).

ascribed to the will of a legally supreme person. It is the plenary faculty which that entity is assumed to possess to express its will in the form of commands legally binding upon all persons over whom it sees fit to claim jurisdiction and with respect to any matters which it may select." [10]

"The exercise of sovereignty is conceived as delegated by a state to the various organs which collectively constitute the government. For practical political reasons which can be easily appreciated, those who determine the public policies of a state ordinarily prefer that these policies should be formulated and executed by governmental agencies of their own creation and which are not subject to the control of other states. There is, however, nothing in the nature of sovereignty or of state life which prevents one state from entrusting the exercise of certain powers to the governmental agencies of another state.... Those governmental agencies thus becoming *quoad hoc* parts of the governmental machinery of the state whose sovereignty is exercised....[11]

"By this delegation the sovereignty of the state which so delegates such powers is not impaired or parted with, for, by legal hypothesis.......it is the will of this state which is expressed, and this state possesses the legal competence again to draw to itself the exercise, through organs of its own creation, of the powers it has granted..." [12]

Kompetenz-Kompetenz. Since the State is thus conceived as being supreme with regard to the choice of its own governing agents it is also considered competent to

[10] p. 197.
[11] pp. 197-198.
[12] p. 198.

determine and limit the function and powers of these agents and of course also the sphere of action of its citizens. As stated by Willoughby:

"It has been seen that when sovereignty is predicated of a state, there is asserted the doctrine that the state is the creator of all the laws in accordance with which its own activities are conducted. In other words, it sets to itself, or rather to its governmental organs and officials, their legal powers. This competency on the part of the state to determine its own legal competency—'Kompetenz-Kompetenz,' as the Germans call it—distinguishes the state from all other human associations of a political or juristic character. The state is supreme, not only as giving the ultimate validity of all the laws which are to fix the rights and obligations of those over whom it chooses to claim jurisdiction, but it is supreme as itself determining the scope of the legal powers of its own governmental agencies and the manner of their exercise. Thus at any one time the domain of the legal and political liberties of the individual is simply that field of interests which the state has willed shall be protected from violation, whether by private persons or public officials....." [13]

From the fundamental premises of this competency of the State to determine the extent of its own powers, i. e. from the so-called Kompetenz-Kompetenz as the German jurists called it, Willoughby deduces a number of propositions which may be briefly given as follows: ".......A state cannot by its own law limit or impair its own sovereignty, it is unable, legally speaking, to decree its own dissolution. An existing government may, by perfectly legal process, transfer its entire powers to another governing machinery, but this does not imply a dissolution of

[13] p. 199.

the state itself. Only when the transfer of authority from one set of governmental agencies to another is effected by illegal, that is, by revolutionary means, can it be said that the old state has gone out of existence and a new one been created....... Whenever there is established a new government whose powers are obtained through constitutional means, no new state is created, however much its powers may differ from those exercised under the old régime. There is only an amendment of the constitution of the old state and a change in its governmental form or policy.... It is sufficiently consistent to say that the old state has been destroyed and a new one created only in those cases in which there has been brought into being what is substantially a new government, or where a new constitution, as a whole, has been put into force in a manner other than that provided for in the old instrument." [14]

"......Sovereignty [according to the definition given to it] has no connection whatever with material or physical power.......It carries with it no implication that there exists in a state the ability actually to enforce those ex-

[14] pp. 200-201. This conclusion Willoughby has modified in his more recent presentation of the doctrine to the effect that: "In this latter case it is perhaps possible to conceive of the State, as organized in its older Government, as going out of existence and a new State as being born with a new Government. But such an interpretation hardly seems necessitated by juristic logic. It would mean that, with the demise of the older sovereignty, all the existing legal rights and duties, public and private, would have to be regarded as destroyed, because the legal basis upon which they had rested would have been removed, and they would then have to be conceived of as impliedly recreated by the new sovereignty. It seems simpler and sufficiently logical to regard the original State as maintaining a continued existence and as having merely given to itself, by an original and direct constitutive act, a new governmental organization." (Fundamental Concepts of Public Law, p. 182). It is this interpretation which is borne out in the prevailing juristic opinion concerning the legal continuity of the German Republican Reich as demonstrated in the writer's work on the Constitutional Jurisprudence of the German Republic.

pressions of its will which, *ex hypothesi,* it has the juristic competence to utter. For the sovereign state knows no limit, whether territorial or personal, to its legislative authority, whereas, of course, every state is in fact limited in the extent of its power not only by the existence of other states, but by the temper and disposition of its own subjects.......As a matter of power, every government depends.......upon public opinion, but this ultimate might of the people is not juristic in character except as it has received formal recognition in law." [15]

State and Government. Reference must finally be made to that part of the theory which emphasizes the distinction between State and Government or between the possession and the exercise of Sovereignty, and the implication of this distinction with regard to the term popular Sovereignty or Sovereignty of the people. As stated in the introduction, the failure to realize this distinction is responsible for most of the misconception of the State and its functions.

"Sovereignty," Willoughby states in part, "inheres in the state as an attribute flowing from its existence as a political person. It therefore is not possessed by any one of its governmental organs or by the government as a whole. This appears when the proper distinction is made between a state and its government; the government exercises, but does not possess, sovereignty. The various governmental organs are but the agencies through which the sovereign will of the state is expressed and carried into execution......." [16]

"The terms, then, 'sovereignty of the people,' 'popular sovereignty,' and 'national sovereignty' cannot accurately

[15] pp. 202-203.
[16] p. 203.

be held to mean that, under the established government, the sovereignty remains in the people. It does mean, however,.......that the constitutional jurisprudence of the state is predicated upon the principle that no person or organ of government is to be regarded as the source whence, by delegation, all other public powers are derived, and as such the residual claimant to all undelegated powers. It furthermore may mean that constitutional provision is made whereby an electorate composed of a considerable portion of the adults of the community, is authorized to perform important functions of government, as, for example, the initiation and ratification of constitutional laws, and in this connection it may be said that in so far as a portion of the people exercises the suffrage for the election or recall of public officials or for the proposing and approval of laws, or for any other public purpose as provided by law, the electorate is to be considered a part of the governmental machinery of the state." [17]

From this definition of the State and Sovereignty it follows that what Austin terms the sovereign action of the British electorate functioning as a limb of the British sovereign body, the King in Parliament; and what Dicey calls the action of the political Sovereign, the British electorate, as distinguished from the acts of the legal Sovereign, Parliament, must be considered as part of the governing activity of the State, i. e. as part of the activity prescribed by the fundamental law of the State. In other words according to the juristic conception of the State the political, i. e. the policy forming function of the executive, the activity of the electorate, partaking at least indirectly of the policy forming character, the application of the laws and determination of their extent and limitation by the judicial department, constitute, each in itself,

[17] p. 205.

only one phase of the manifestation or exercise of the sovereign will of the State. As such they are each every one of them subject to regulation and control in accordance with the terms of the fundamental law of the body politic as embodied in the constitution.

Sovereignty and International Law. The theory of the juristic personality of the State as thus developed by Willoughby is predicated upon the monistic doctrine of the supremacy of municipal over international law in the sense that the latter is not law in the proper meaning of the word, i. e. not positive law, or else it is based upon the dualistic doctrine which, though conceding the legal character of international obligation, insists upon the independence of the one from the other, or at least upon the independence of municipal law from the law of nations. Concerning this point Willoughby writes:

"As regards their origin, the laws of international life do not find their birth in the mandatory utterances of supreme wills declaring to inferior persons what for them shall be deemed legally right and legally wrong. Instead, law appears as stating rules of action which derive their force from the fact that they have been accepted by those political persons—the states—whose actions they are to regulate. This acceptance may, indeed, be one which, for the most part, the states may not find it practicable to avoid, even should they so desire; and thus, in fact, the rules of international law may, *arguendo,* be admitted to be as definite, and, in general, as uniformly conformed to, as are the provisions of the municipal law of the most orderly state. This, however, does not change the essential character of these international laws as rules which obtain between equals rather than as commands addressed by a superior legislative will to persons who are conceived of as subject to its control.[18]

"Even when, by formal treaties, independent states have established rules by which, with reference to the matters specified their future dealings with one another are to be regulated, there has been no creation of law in a positive or Austinian sense, for, as to those matters, the contracting parties remain subject only to their own wills and not to that of an outside or foreign power......." [19]

On the basis of this interpretation of international law Willoughby holds that: "It would plainly appear that the idea of sovereignty as it is found in constitutional law can find no proper place among international conceptions...." In the sphere of international relations the term " 'independency'......far better than 'sovereignty' would indicate the fact that, regarded from the point of view of positive law, complete individualism prevails in the international field.......This being so, in order to build up a science of international relations, it is necessary to begin with a conception of the State that will correspond to the conditions to which it is to be applied." [20]

Concerning the definition of the State in the field of international relations Willoughby concludes that "from the nature of the case this conception must be something different from that of the constitutional state. Like the constitutional state, it must be viewed as a political person or entity possessing and expressing a will of its own and operating through an instrumentality termed a 'government.' But this will cannot be conceived of as a legal will, nor as a will supreme over the other state-persons to

[18] pp. 206-207.
[19] p. 207.
[20] pp. 207-208.

whom it is addressed. And, of course, the expressions of its will, whatever actual force they may have behind them, cannot be regarded as laws in a strictly juristic sense. So different, then, are these two fields of constitutional and international law, that nothing but confusion can result from an attempt to employ concepts in the one field appropriate only in the other. Especially does it seem desirable that the strictly legal concept of 'sovereignty,' which constitutes the fundamental idea in constitutional jurisprudence, should not find a permanent lodgment in international terminology......"[21]

[21] p. 208.

CHAPTER VII.

Criticism of the Theory

State and Sovereignty from the Constitutional Aspect. In the following account of the criticism of the juristic conception of the State as expounded by Willoughby, we shall follow the author's presentation of his theory, dealing first with the criticism of the doctrine in its constitutional, and second in its international legal aspect. In the opinion of Willoughby's critics the theory offers difficulties chiefly on five scores which are pointedly summarized in the following quotations.[1]

The first difficulty is historical in so far as "Professor Willoughby does not seem.......sufficiently to recognize that the view he expounds took its rise in a special set of historical circumstances and has neither application nor meaning outside them." Thus the critic contends "it has no validity.......in the whole of the middle ages; it would in fact, have been repudiated with horror by every respectable mediæval publicist" and "it is also probable

[1] These quotations are taken from Harold J. Laski's review of Willoughby's Fundamental Concepts of Public Law. In this connection see also the criticism of the juristic conception of the State by Ellen Deborah Ellis which appeared as the manuscript of the present work was going to press (Political Science at the Crossroads. American Political Science Review, vol. XXI, 1927, pp. 773-791). "Political Science at the Crossroads" contains not only an able review of the theory in question, but it offers most interesting constructive suggestions for the rehabilitation of political science in general and of the juristic conception of the State in particular. As understood by the writer the essential thesis is this: Greater emphasis upon the pre-natal existence of the juristic person called State and upon the political as distinguished from the formalistic or legal aspect of State and Sovereignty would on the one hand tend to allay the criticism of the a-

that as the nation-State ceases to be the ultimate unit of social organization it will cease to have contemporary applicability......."

The second difficulty is that "if it [the juristic conception of the State] alone is to be accepted as scientific there are many social units today acting as States in every practical sense of the word which, because they cannot be confined within the four corners of Professor Willoughby's definitions, cease to be States. That is....... (despite the remarks of Professor Willoughby at p. 249 *et seq.*) true of the United States; it is true of Belgium; it is true, also, of the new Germany."

In the third place objection is raised to the theory as not being realistic. Referring to Willoughby's own admission that on grounds of one sort or another, sovereign authorities are not free to make law as they please, the reader is put to the question: "Is a jurisprudence the concepts of which are so remote from practical life likely to do us real service? Is it not better frankly to admit that, on the contrary, a scientific jurisprudence must, if it is to be truly scientific, be written in terms of the total social environment it will encounter?"

social and a-moral nature of the State as conceived by the analytical jurist, and on the other hand serve to clarify the relation between Sovereignty and law as purely formalistic concepts posited as a result of mere metaphysical speculation and political power and physical force as the practical and categorical imperatives of the realities of all social and State life. The suggestions implied have been dealt with in the present work, especially in chapter VIII (Vinogradoff's modification of the juristic conception of the State), chapter IX (The denial of Sovereignty by Duguit, Laski and others), and in the writer's Principles of Constitutional Jurisprudence of the German National Republic (to appear as companion volume to the present work), particularly in Chapter IV dealing with the question of the legal continuity of the Republican Reich.

The fourth objection seems to be practically identical with the preceding one. "Professor Willoughby's view," we are told, "would reduce jurisprudence to a mere anatomy, where, to be creative, it ought to be a physiology." For "in practically every case where we deal with law, we are watching a governmental process. The thing of importance in that process is the system of purposes and consequences by which it is informed. The view maintained by Professor Willoughby abstracts altogether this system of law, and argues that the only thing the lawyer has to consider is the question of whether it has in fact originated from the properly competent source. This seems to...... deprive jurisprudence of any contact whatever with life," and the critic does "not believe that it can live without that contact."

A fifth and final difficulty is found in Willoughby's contention that "the legal theory of sovereignty does not assign to the supreme authority any moral pre-eminence of any kind." Conceding that this "is, of course, formally true," objection is made from the point of view of political reality. "Practically, it seems to me [the critic] undeniable that a position of legal pre-eminence results (however unjustifiably) in the tacit assumption of moral superiority.......For the State has to act through persons; and those who are its guests [guides, agents] at a given moment are always convinced that they are acting in the name of eternal justice. I do not believe that the history of States supports that conviction and I am therefore anxious to deny a philosophy which, as I believe, supplies it with its protective armor." Pointing to the alleged consequences of this state of affairs, the critic "would add that a peculiarly flagrant example of the consequences of this view is to be found in the history of State liability for tortious acts. Professor Willoughby, with the powerful support of Mr. Justice Holmes in *Kawananokoa* v. *Polyblank* (205 U. S. 349), is able, of course, to maintain that the denial of liability is merely a matter of formal logic. He [Willoughby] does not add that it is a formal logic the results of which are often unfair, and sometimes disastrous, to those who suffer from it. That is a type of formal logic not very satisfactory in its operation."

Analysis of the Preceding Criticism. In the first place it is held that Willoughby's theory does not sufficiently take into consideration the fact that the view as expounded by him arose in a special set of historical data, that consequently it does not apply to the States of the middle ages, and that finally, it may not apply to the time when the *civitas maxima* will come into being and the present nation-State will cease to be the unit body politic. This criticism and the answer to be given, involve the question whether on the one hand political theory is purely the result of speculation upon historically given facts—in other words, whether, applying the mechanistic interpretation of the biologist, we look upon historical data as a kind of political germ plasm which produces political theory very much as the biological organism is held to produce thought by way of a chemical activity—or whether, on the other hand, speculation in the sphere of things politic is to be considered as a sort of vitalistic force which animates and to some extent controls the growth and particular development of the protoplasmic social and political entities destined or striving to become nations and States. The statement that Willoughby's doctrine is the result of speculation on certain historical facts and as such not applicable to the States of the middle ages is clearly predicated upon a mechanistic interpretation, while the rejection of the theory as incompatible with the critic's own conception of the future world-State,[2] seems to imply with equal force that in this instance the critic chooses to draw upon the vitalistic interpretation in support of his contention. Admitting that political thought may in some cases or to some extent be the driving force and creative element in the establishment of historical facts, while in other cases and to the same extent it may be the result of given historical data, we fail to see why a theory which unquestionably in the preponderant opinion of modern authorities, applies to the existing State organizations, should be rejected because it is inapplicable first to historical conditions no longer existant, and second, to a state of affairs, desired by some or many, but not yet a reality. The same is true of the second difficulty, i. e. that Willoughby's theory does not apply to such States as the United States, Belgium and especially the new Germany. Willoughby's theory, as understood and interpreted by the writer, applies without any difficulty whatsoever, to the United States, to Belgium and above all to the new Germany, the latter of which has constructed its constitutional organization squarely upon the juristic conception of the State, as will appear from Chapter XI and from the writer's examination of this question in the "Principles of the Constitutional Jurisprudence of the German National Republic." The applicability of the juristic conception of the State under the future world-State will be considered in detail in connection with a review of the so-called Austrian or Viennese School which posits the Sovereignty of the *civitas maxima* and that of international law over the law of the nation-State and which thus denies the Sovereignty of the State as conceived in the interpretation of the juristic conception of the State as here adopted.

[2] A Grammar of Politics....1925, especially chapter XI (International Organization).

What seems to constitute the greatest obstacle to the correct understanding of the juristic conception of the State is contained in the third and fourth difficulties to the effect that the concepts of Willoughby's jurisprudence are too remote from practical life to do us real service; that it would be better frankly to admit a scientific jurisprudence, to be truly scientific, should be written in terms of the total social environment it will encounter. This criticism is based upon the fact that "sovereign authorities are not free to make law as they please......." and that "they are the creatures either of convention or custom which they dare not violate." Willoughby's view would, in the critic's opinion, reduce jurisprudence to an anatomy, where it should be a physiology; it would deprive jurisprudence of that contact with life without which it cannot live.

Before we consider this criticism in detail we must call attention to the fact that Willoughby, apparently foreseeing the difficulty on this score, gave solemn warning to reader and critic "to bear steadily in mind: that the doctrine of sovereignty that is developed in this study, is a purely juristic one, and, therefore, that the attribute of omnipotence which is ascribed to the sovereign State in no way implies that the actual power of the State has no limits, or that those who influence or control the policies of the State may disregard the obligations which ethical justice and right impose." This warning is not only found in the body of his various works on the subject, i. e. The Nature of the State, The Juristic Conception of the State, The Fundamental Concepts of Public Law, but is given prominence in the preface of the last work cited where the author adds "care is taken in the body of the work to enter this *caveat,* but, because of its importance, it is also stated here." We are thus confronted with the necessity of searching for the basic reason for the failure to dissociate, despite this warning, the concepts of legal omnipotence and practical limitations, resulting in the charge that the admission of practical limitation renders useless the idea of legal omnipotence. However, since the question involved in this issue plays an important part also in Professor Vinogradoff's attempted modification of the juristic conception of the State, it will be more profitably considered in connection with the discussion of Vinogradoff's modification of the doctrine.[3]

The same procedure will prove best suited to the analysis of the fifth and final objection, to wit, that there is a contradiction in the position taken by Willoughby who, on the one hand, denies the legal liability of the State for tortious acts, and, on the other hand, stresses the fact that this denial of liability is merely a matter of formal logic, failing, however, to add that "it is a formal logic the results of which are often unfair, and sometimes disastrous, to those who suffer from it." As Vinogradoff ventures to overcome the difficulty here voiced by positing the legal liability of the State it seems preferable to consider also this phase of the criticism in connection with Vinogradoff's version of the juristic conception of the State.[4]

State and Sovereignty from the International Aspect. For a criticism of the juristic conception of the State from the point of view of international law we must refer to Professor Crane's discussion of Willoughby's presentation of the doctrine in the article published in the American Political Science Review.[5] Starting with a reference to Willoughby's warning that his theory be taken only as a formalistic system and that the positing of legal omnipo-

[3] See next chapter.

[4] *Ibid.*

[5] Crane, Discussion. American Political Science Review, vol. XII, 1918, pp. 209-214.

tence does not preclude political or ethical limitations of the State, Crane proceeds in part as follows:

"This formalism of the analytical school is unacceptable to many minds. It is objected that its theories do not square with the actual facts of life. The ground on which this objection is based could not be more clearly stated than by Dr. Willoughby. He has deduced with inexorable logic from the analytical theory the corollary that the human individuals who are the subjects of a state are determined by a mere exercise of the law-making power. Any state may by a simple fiat of the sovereign make every inhabitant of the globe its subject. With equal logic it follows that in precisely the same territory and over precisely the same individuals there may exist two or more sovereignties or states.

"Such conclusions seem repugnant to common sense. A sovereignty that rests upon a mere formal assertion seems totally lacking in reality. It is an empty form, a form without substance. If logic leads to the deduction from the analytical theory that the entire population of the world can be embraced in the people of a state by a mere fiat of the sovereign, that theory can hardly be said to square with a sound general theory of politics." [6]

"This objection," Crane holds, "appears on solid ground, and calls for some amendment of the analytical theory." His amendment is in effect this: The analytical school defines positive law as a command from the sovereign to subject. But does the command of the sovereign, i. e. the State, address itself to the subject? Is it not possible to conceive of law as a command not addressed to the subject but to the governing agents of State? In order to answer this question in a positive sense Crane defines law

[6] *Ibid.*, pp. 210-212.

as a command directed to "human individuals as the subject matter within which it operates, not as subject intelligences to which it is addressed." He considers law in the analytical sense "not as a command to a subject, but as a mere statement of cause and effect, somewhat like a natural physical law." According to this definition "law.... is addressed by the sovereign to its own agents" and "to these it is, as a matter of fact, supreme." According to Crane, "only by shifting the incidence of the command from the subjects to the governmental agencies, can the assertion of the analytical school that the whole world may be made subject to any state by the mere fiat of its law be reconciled with fact. Only with such an alteration of the incidence of the command, does it seem possible to agree with Dr. Willoughby when he says: '.......all persons, whatever their political relations and affiliations, are potentially subject to the legal control of a given state....' " Crane's argument does not eliminate the difficulty complained of, it merely changes its character or aspect. In the first place, the definition of law as a command directed not to the subject but only to the State's agents is untenable. Law in the positive sense does not only aim at the punishment of the culprit by the State's agencies, but also at the prevention of crime on the part of the subject. In the second place, if it is incongruous for the State to bring under its control, by its simple legal fiat, the subjects of other States, it must be equally incongruous for the State to expect its agents to carry out its commands outside of its own territorial limits, that is within the sphere subject to the legal control of other States. The difficulty to which Crane quite properly calls attention may be appreciated more easily and probably admitted more readily if we discard for a moment the technical language in which the problem is presented. Stating the case in the language of the ordinary man we are here confronted with the all-penetrating bullet meeting the impenetrable armor. If the twain meet, only one can live up to its reputation. But the failure of either in one test does not preclude a reversal of the result of the first meeting in a later test. Applied to the actualities of political life this means that constitutional law, fortified by international usage, convention, or law, whatever we may call it, has always upheld, and still upholds the right of conquest, or rather of acquisition of territory from one State to another. On the other hand, the same constitutional law, equally supported by international theory and practice, upholds the right of every State to defend itself against the loss of its territory by way of conquest on the part of another State.

As thus stated the problem suggests the astonishing conclusion that what is untenable in the proposition is not the assertion of the formal legal omnipotence of the State with regard to other States, but the criticism of this assertion on the basis that it does not conform to the practical side of inter-State relations, and that as such seems "repugnant to common sense." It is true, this phase of the legal omnipotence of the State is real only to the extent to which one State can actually impose its fiat upon the other, but to that extent is a quite drastic actuality for the successful as well as for the unsuccessful rival in the contest of legal wills. The assertion of the formal legal omnipotence of the State, un-moral as it may be, must be accepted as in conformity with political reality, as long as conquest and cession of territory against the will of the ceding State is sanctioned by international law. It is not until the time comes when international morality will refuse its sanction to such a practice, that the allegation of the formal legal omnipotence of the State, in the sense in which it is here discussed, can be properly termed repugnant to common sense. But when that time comes the difficulty referred to will be solved not by Crane's change in the definition of law but by the re-examintion of the premises upon which the assertion of such legal omnipotence rests. If or when international law establishes the sanctity or inviolability of a State's territory, we may well limit Sovereignty, conceived as the legal will of the State, to the internationally recognized territory upon which the citizenry forming the body politic resides and enjoys its political existence. The extra territorial activities of the State now exercised on the ground of a formal legal right will then be carried out purely on the basis of the comity of nations or under the formal sanction of international law.[7]

But even as matters stand today the assertion of the formal legal omnipotence of the State will not seem quite so incompatible with the common sense view of the most critical observer if we establish the proper meaning of the term omnipotence. The word omnipotence, like omniscience, is an expression employed by man to denote a characteristic or attribute of the infinite being called God. As thus used it represents to the human mind the idea of the total absence of all limitation practical as well as formal. Is it logical and compatible with common sense to apply the same term with the same meaning to the State, that is, to a finite institution? Is not the term omnipotence when employed in connection with the State merely intended to describe a certain degree or condition of relativity of competence pertaining to the State in preference to other institutions which are not States? And if so, does

[7] In this connection see James W. Garner, Limitations on National Sovereignty in International Relations (American Political Science Review, vol. XIX, 1925, pp. 1-24). The relation of the juristic conception of the State to the doctrine of the supremacy of international law will be considered in more detail in chapters X-XIII.

not any criticism of the allegation of the formal legal omnipotence of the State constitute an indictment, not only of the assertion of such omnipotence, but of the very conception of the State as a juristic person, and of Sovereignty as its essential attribute? As a matter of fact the more relentless, because more consistent, critics such as Laski and Duguit, have actually extended their objection to the point of denying the legal personality of the State and the existence of Sovereignty as a necessary attribute of the body politic. This phase of the problem will be examined in the chapter dealing with the denial of Sovereignty by Laski, Duguit and others.

CHAPTER VIII.

Vinogradoff's Modification of the Theory

The State and Law. The juristic conception of the State as defined in the preceding chapters starts with the *de facto* organization of society as a body politic. It does not, therefore, concern itself with a justification of the State beyond that given in the terms of its definition. Accepting the will of this body politic as the law of the State the same doctrine has no need of deducing the source of law from an authority outside or above the State itself. The attempts made to establish a justification of the State beyond the one given in the above definition, and the insistence upon a source of law other than the State, have produced a number of theories, none of which can be accepted as being generally applicable to the modern State or to the prevailing theories of our legal systems.[1]

An interesting demonstration of this fact is found in an article on the "Juridical Nature of the State" by the late Sir Paul Vinogradoff.[2] In this study the author, apparently under the influence of Professor Brown,[3] starts with the proposition that "Sovereignty cannot be considered as something given once for all, so that it may be consigned for its application to a general and abstract jurisprudence." He holds that "in order to understand the working of that idea of Sovereignty we have to distinguish at least between three stages." The first was the feudal stage

[1] For a review and analysis of the earlier attempts of this kind see Willoughby, The Nature of the State, p. 184; Fundamental Concepts of Public Law, p. 166 ff.

[2] Michigan Law Review, vol. XXIII, 1924, pp. 138-153.

[3] See chapter V, note 10.

with the contractual basis of ruler and ruled. In this stage Sovereignty was considered "as an *object of right.*" The second stage was the period of absolutism as exemplified by the French monarchy absorbing the feudal estates and lords. This stage, Vinogradoff holds, was glorified by Hobbes and Spinoza and is expounded even today in the text books of the Austinian school.[4] In this stage the State was and is conceived as *"the dominant subject of right."* The third or modern stage, according to Vinogradoff, is one in which "thought is directed towards a goal in which the State has no unlimited power of doing what it pleases." In this third stage the modern State is conceived as a "legal State." It "is not only a creation of force, it is also an embodiment of law: as such it is a subject of duties as well as of rights."[5] The theory of the legal origin of the State, so Vinogradoff argues, has been based at various times upon various conceptions as to source or character of law. The Roman world placed law above the State on the ground that the source of all law was to be found in the dictates of natural reason as conceived by the Stoics.[6] In the theory of medieval canon law, natural reason became divine or natural law. Vinogradoff points to the recrudescence of the resort to natural law or natural reason as the superior of positive law in modern times. "In the 20th Century," he writes, "the view that law as the social sense of right is above the State is emphatically expressed, e. g., by a Dutch writer, Krabbe, whose work has been lately translated into English.[7] He [Krabbe] comes to the conclusion that the State cannot be entrusted with the formation of the right law. If the rule of law has to be considered as its chief attribute then

[4] Vinogradoff, p. 140 ff.

[5] Ibid., pp. 141-142.

[6] Cicero, De Republica (cited *ibid.*, p. 146).

[7] The Modern Idea of the State, tr. by Sabine....1922.

law must be derived from something higher than the State. Law 'is the summing up of the valuation which we make as a result of our mental capacities.' We are constantly valuing things, we value them by law and ethical judgment. 'For authority of law is to be sought in the reaction of the feeling for right. This authority, therefore, lies within a man and not outside him.....'."[8]

As Vinogradoff points out, it is easy to find the weak point of such a position. The sense of right of which Krabbe speaks is, of course, public opinion. But who are the recognized mouthpieces who have to formulate and to put into force the rules expressing this sense of right? "No personal function," Vinogradoff answers, "can be imagined without personal agents to carry it out: the State would appear as the *juridical person responsible for carrying out the function of formulating,* applying and enforcing law," i. e. the law of which the State is not the source but merely the formulating agent.[9]

But what is Vinogradoff's alternative to his rejection of the doctrine that the State is the source of positive law and of Krabbe's theory positing the source of law outside the State? It is this that on the whole the State and law seem to be *"two aspects of the same thing."* Law he defines as "the regulation of Society considered as the aggregate of its rules," the State as "the organization of Society considered as the personal agency responsible for its organization."[10]

[8] Vinogradoff, pp. 146-147.

[9] *Ibid.*, p. 147.

[10] The same theory was for a time held by Kelsen: "The State character of law and the legal character of the State constitute materially nothing different; they are only different sides of the same medal, the essential (Kernpunkt) is the substantial not the formal identity of law and State" (Hauptprobleme der Staatsrechtslehre, 1911, p. 253). In the preface to the second edition of 1923 this statement is quoted for the purpose of showing its failure to grasp the real character of

The State as Subject of Legal Rights and Duties. With Vinogradoff's concept of law no fault need be found. His definition of the State, however, is not compatible with the juristic theory of the State as propounded by Willoughby and applicable to the modern State. Vinogradoff, as we have seen, is equally emphatic in his rejection of all theories which seek for the source of law outside and above the State, as well as of those which define the State as being the source of law and being itself not subject to law. He holds that the modern State can no longer be considered as possessing unlimited power to do what it pleases. It must be conceived as the legal State in the sense that it is the subject not only of rights but also of duties. But in his attempt to posit absolute legal limitations of the State he naturally and inevitably falls into the old error of injecting into his concept of the "legal State" the personal element of the magistracy representing what he considers the aspect of the legal organization of society. It is on the basis of this ambiguity that he defines the State as "the organization of Society considered as the personal agency responsible for its organization," or as the *"Juridical person responsible for carrying out the function of formulating,* applying and enforcing law." It is this apparent confusion of State and Government or governing magistracy which leads Vinogradoff to the assertion that the State is the subject of legal rights and duties, a proposition definitely denied by Willoughby. As we shall see below, it is on the basis of the same failure to distinguish between the concepts of State and Government that Laski

the legal aspect of the State which Kelsen in this connection defines as the complete identity of State and Law, "The State," he says, "as the subject of juristic cognition (Erkenntnis) can be only law because to perceive juristically and to comprehend legally, is the same as to conceive something as law (Recht)" (Hauptprobleme....1923, p. xvii). See also chapter X (Kelsen's Concept of the State as a Juristic Person).

criticised Willoughby's position as the product "of a formal logic the results of which are often unfair, and sometimes disastrous, to those who suffer from it," inasmuch as "a peculiarly flagrant example of the consequences of this view is to be found in the history of State liability for tortious acts." [11]

While it is unfortunately true that the constitutional law of some States, including that of the United States, rejects the doctrine of the State's liability for tortious acts of its governing agents, such rejection is by no means dictated by the tenets of the juristic conception of the State, properly understood. As a matter of fact, the principle of legal responsibility of the State for the illegal acts of its governing agents has been definitely accepted in continental European constitutional theory and practice. It is a well known fact that until recently French constitutional theory and practice denied such responsibility on the part of the State. But it should be equally well known that there has been in France, during the last two decades, a complete reversal of the former position. In a decision of Jan. 4, 1918, the French administrative court (Conseil d'État) stated that there could be no question of the legal responsibility of the State in case of losses inflicted upon private citizens by public officials when negligence or fault on the part of the official or the public service is proven. In a decision of Feb. 17, 1905, the Conseil d'État said that the State might be held responsible even where no particular fault of the service could be established.[12]

[11] See chapter VII (State and Sovereignty from the Constitutional Aspect).

[12] See Revue du droit public et de la science politique en France et à l'étranger....vol. 35, 1918, pp. 403-405; vol. 27, 1910, p. 72 ff. The question of the legal obligations of the State has been dealt with in R. Dorsey Watkins' timely study: The State as Party Litigant....The Johns Hopkins Press, 1927.

The principle of a limited responsibility of the State has been applied in German constitutional practice since the middle of the nineteenth century. By the so-called Tumultschadengesetz of March 11, 1850,[13] Prussia had recognized the legal responsibility of the State for damage done to private citizens in consequence of internal disturbances. By the Law of May 12, 1920 (Gesetz über die durch innere Unruhen verursachten Schäden),[14] the German Republic recognized the same obligation. On May 22, 1910, the Empire, by the Law concerning the obligation of the Reich for the actions of its functionaries,[15] established legal responsibility of the State for damages or losses inflicted upon private citizens by officials (Beamte) of the Empire. Similar legal provisions existed prior to the revolution in most of the German States.[16] Article I, Section 1 of the Federal law of May 12, 1910, has been embodied almost literally in Article 131 of the German National Republican Constitution of 1919. In the case of the German practice, however, State responsibility is limited to such damages as are the result of *ultra vires* action of the State's agents concerned.[17]

[13] Gesetz vom. 11. März, 1850, betreffend die Verpflichtung der Gemeinden zum Ersatz des bei öffentlichen Aufläufen verursachten Schadens. (Gesetz-Sammlung für die königlich Preussischen Staaten, 1806 bis 1883 incl., bd. II, 1841-1854, p. 284).

[14] Sammlung von Reichsgesetzen....Hrsg. von Dr. Carl Sartorius.... 5 ed., 1921, p. 547 ff.

[15] *Ibid.*, p. 389 ff.

[16] See Meyer-Anschütz, p. 612 ff.

[17] There have been a number of decisions of the German courts upholding the individual's rights under these State liability acts in cases where some of the States involved disclaimed their liability.

In a decision of July 8, 1920 the Reichsgericht, agreeing with the lower State courts ruled that the *ultra vires* character of the action complained of must be proved. In the case in question plaintiff sued for compensation for damage inflicted to his houses. The damage had been caused by the firing of shots by members of the Soldiers' Councils stationed as guards at the railway station of Frankfort. The Reichs-

The French and German practice here referred to unquestionably establishes a responsibility of the State for certain damages inflicted upon the private citizen by the actions of the State's agents. This obligation is of a legal character, i. e. an obligation determined by the law and subject to enforcement by legal methods. But this determination and execution, though taking place in the name of the State is actually accomplished and effected by certain organs or agents of the State. In other words while the State through National law or constitutional provisions assumes for itself this obligation, in doing so

gericht declared that the members of the Soldiers' Councils had acted within their legal right in using their fire arms (RGZ. vol. 100, p. 255 ff).

In a decision of July 13, 1920, the Reichsgericht, overruling a verdict of the lower State courts, declared that the expropriation and sale by one of the Soldiers' Councils of the private property legally acquired by a soldier, and the application of the proceeds of the sale to the liquidation of the soldier's alleged indebtedness, to constitute an *ultra vires* act under the State liability laws of the Reich (RGZ. vol. 100, p. 285 ff).

State liability under the liability acts concerned extends not only to private persons injured by a civil service official but also to injuries suffered by one State official in consequence of the *ultra vires* action of another. In 1922 the State Court of Hanover dismissed as not justiciable the case of a postal telegraph employee who was suing the Reich for back pay due him by reason of deferred promotion. Having twice requested admission to a certain examination he had twice been denied that admission on the basis of alleged untruthful reports by his superior official. Succeeding in a third attempt he passed the examination and received the promotion sought. He then sued the Reich for the difference in salary involved. The Reichsgericht, overruling the State court, stated that the plaintiff was not basing his action on the refusal of the authorities to admit him to the examination in question, but upon the allegation of untruthful reports of his superior, in consequence of which the authorities refused his admission to the examination. On this ground, the Reichsgericht ruled, his case was clearly justiciable (RGZ. vol. 105, pp. 196-198).

In this connection see the author's Principles of Constitutional Jurisprudence of the German National Republic, chapter XIV, sections dealing with fundamental rights and police power.

it merely instructs some of its agencies, let us say the courts, to determine the existence and extent of a certain financial or other material liability to be met by another agency of the State, let us say the treasury, for the damages accruing to a private citizen or for that matter, to any third party, from the actions of the State's functionaries.

The only legally binding effect then of such assumption on the part of the State is one of holding the particular agencies designated to the performance of the duties placed upon them by the particular formulation which such an assumption of responsibility has taken. As far as the State itself is concerned, there is no legal agency within the State nor, at the present time, outside of it, which could either force the State to assume such a responsibility or, after it has been assumed, to prevent its abrogation. As far as the German States and the German Federal Union are concerned the assumption of such responsibility was an act of political expediency forced upon the constitutional agencies concerned as a result of the revolutionary uprisings of 1848 and 1849, by political pressure brought to bear in 1910, and by the effort to repair as far as possible the material damage wrought by the revolutionary movement of 1918. In France such obligation was accepted in consequence of the general opposition manifesting itself since the beginning of the twentieth century against the over centralization of the governmental machinery and the unbearably bureaucratic attitude of the State functionary, as will be shown below in connection with the examination of Duguit's denial of Sovereignty, which constitutes one of the phases of this opposition.

It is only within the limitations of the above explanation that we can accept Vinogradoff's statement that the

State is the subject of legal rights and duties. The same limitation applies, of course, to the contrary position taken by Willoughby. Under the heading "The State not a Subject of Legal Rights and Obligation," the latter, admitting that there is some dispute among jurists as to this question, writes, "if, however, the viewpoint of the analytical jurist is rigidly adhered to, there would seem to be no difficulty in asserting the negative upon this point." "The State," he continues, "being regarded as itself the source of law, cannot be regarded as bound by the obligations which that law creates; and, even as to rights, the ascription of them to the State is meaningless, since their continuance as well as their creation, their character, and their content, are wholly subject to the State's will....." But he adds: "It scarcely need be said that this denial of legal rights and duties has reference only to the State and not to its various governmental organs or officials. These, as has been earlier pointed out, have their competences determined by law, and, therefore, they must, at least in every constitutionally organized State, be regarded as the possessors of legal rights and as the subjects of legal obligations....." Clear as this passage must seem to those who are willing to see, it does contain an ambiguity for those who prefer the attitude of the critic. To state that "the State, being regarded as itself the source of law, cannot be regarded as bound by the obligations which that law creates.....," is of course correct only on the supposition that it cannot thus be considered bound in a legal way. In other words, there cannot be said to exist within the State an agency which can in a manner in which laws are enforced, hold the State, i. e. the nation organized as a body politic, to the observation of that law. But this does not mean that there is no other way in which the State can be said to be bound to that obligation, once assumed. The most uncompromising advocate of the juristic conception of the State, must for the sake of the integrity of his own position assert with the utmost emphasis that the State has a very practical, i. e. a moral obligation to abide by the consequences of its own law as long as this law is formally in existence. The failure on the part of Society, politically organized and conceived as a legal person, called the State, to recognize and submit to the sanctions of its own law is of course not followed like that of the individual by a verdict in a civil or criminal court, or in a court martial. But the punishment for this sin against the Holy Ghost of politics is no less certain than that awaiting the individual's disregard of the law of the land. A nation flouting its own formal law by a general disrespect and disregard of the obligations assumed by that law, cannot be fined, imprisoned or sent to a mass grave, but it will, under the weight of its own guilt slowly descend to that point of disintegration where it must cease to be a National or political unit fit to maintain itself against its more consistent, because more self-respecting neighbors. It is this aspect of the question of the State's subjectivity to rights and duties, embodied in the quotation from Laski's review of the "Fundamental Concepts of Public Law" constituting the last of the five difficulties referred to in Chapter VII, which is at the base of the criticism of Willoughby's view on this subject. What is criticised there is not in reality Willoughby's denial of the formal legal binding force of the State's obligations or legal responsibility, but the failure of some States, as for instance the United States, to realize the desirability of assuming a morally and practically binding responsibility for the *ultra vires* or all acts of its functionaries, resulting in damage to the private citizen or to any third party affected by such acts. It is this same aspect of the question which leads us to the last phase of Vinogradoff's modification of the theory of the juristic conception of the State, i. e. the one dealing with the doctrine in its relation to the realities of political life in general, manifested in the pressure and influence of public opinion as a medium of extra-legal sanction.

The State and Extra-legal Sanctions. On the basis of the preceding definitions of the law of the State and of the State as a subject of legal rights and duties, etc., Vinogradoff summarizes what he considers the modern juridical nature of the State in the following three main propositions, to wit: "(I). The State is a society legally organized for the protection of social intercourse. (II). The principal legal attribute of the State is sovereignty in the sense of finality of decision in the formulation of legal rules and in their application. (III). For the enforcement of legal rules the State relies on *sanctions,* which are partly legal compulsion and partly extra-legal appeal to society at large in the form of pressure of public opinion and, in extreme cases, to the direct action of social forces." [18]

Reference has been made to the fact that elements of actual power, moral right or political expediency have been specifically excluded from the formal definition of the State and Sovereignty under the juristic theory as presented above. As already pointed out, it is the fact of the exclusion of these elements which constitutes the chief difficulty in the way of an acceptance of Willoughby's juristic conception of the State. It is true, Willoughby states that the definition of Sovereignty, i. e. Sovereignty conceived as the legal will of the State, connotes a purely legal competence or jurisdiction in which "no element of actual power (as distinguished from will), or of moral

[18] Vinogradoff, p. 153.

right, or of political expediency, is involved." [19] However, this should not be interpreted to mean that the juristic conception of the State, as here accepted, denies the existence of these elemental and practical forces in the life of the body politic. It would be futile to deny that actual force, moral ideas, i. e. so-called notions of right and wrong, and considerations of expediency or practicability, played an important part in the original *de facto* transformation of society into a body politic or State, or that these same forces continue to play the same rôle in the actual life of the State, once it has come into existence. But elements of force, conceptions of right and wrong, as well as influence of political expediency are purely subjective and variable qualities or quantities. This being so, the theory of the juristic conception of the State envisages their application in accordance with definite and legally binding norms by a determinate set of functionaries held responsible to the body politic for the observation of such application. In other words, these elements are considered primarily not as recognized legal functions, but as ways and means toward the realization of legal action, i. e. ways and means prescribed by law for the maintenance of the law.

This, however, is only the formal and ideal aspect of the matter, which from a purely practical point of view is far too formal and ideal to account for the actual resort to force based upon particular notions of right or wrong and political expediency in a manner incompatible with the formal law of the State. It is for this reason that the adherent of the juristic conception of the State, though he may exclude these elements from the purely formal definition of Sovereignty, must take care not to ignore their existence and the importance of the rôle played by them

[19] See chapter VI, note 7.

in the application of extra-legal as well as of legal sanctions in the enforcement of the law of the State. As will be admitted by both follower and critic of the juristic conception of the State, the legal control over the definite or determinate set of functionaries acting as the State's agents for the execution of the business of the body politic is only a formal one. To speak, as we do, of the will of the State as an abstraction of the cumulative wills of the individuals forming the State, as the will of the majority, or as the will of the actual number of those participating in the formulation of that will, is a rather naive way of attempting a definition of something which does not allow of a definition, because it is too changeable and elusive to be put in the strait-jacket of human words expressing definite and determinable notions or facts. The assumed will of the body politic has in the past and present been established in a number of ways. In the theocratic State of the Orient, and for that matter in every autocracy, it is manifested by the ruler representing the deity and deriving his right to rulership from that source. In the democratic Greek city State, it was formulated by the universal vote of the free citizens. In the early Germanic tribes it was ascertained in general periodical meetings at which all the armed freemen of the tribe convened. The same primitive method still prevails *mutatis mutandis,* in some of the Swiss cantons, and, for the regulation of local affairs in other democratic States.[20] But in the modern extended nation-State the will of the State is formulated by a definitely limited number of citizens and officials. The number varies according to the classification of the State's government as democratic or non-democratic. Not

[20] On this subject see the author's The Employment of the Plebiscite in the Determination of Sovereignty, pp. 12-20, 196-198; also the chapter dealing with Ordinances in the work on German constitutional jurisprudence referred to in note 17.

only the number of those qualified in the formulation of the will may thus vary, but also the method of formulation differs greatly. What is more important and significant still is the fact that where a definite number of citizens and officials has been designated for the act of formulating the State's will, those actually participating in the act of this formulation may constitute only a fraction of those legally qualified to do so. It is the result of this formulation as established or sanctioned by the judgment or *libitum* of each particular political society, which we accept as the sovereign will of the State and which we must accept as such as long as we tolerate the particular method by which it has been formulated. It must, of course, be admitted that the law thus formulated and accepted as the supreme will of the State is, considered from the point of view of reality, nothing but a variable approximation of what we optimistically choose to call the will of the people or nation. The same applies to all State action. The body politic can transact its business only through human agencies. All the acts of these human agencies are to be conducted in accordance with legal norms set down by the body politic for their guidance. But human action contains an element which cannot be brought under formal legal control, such as man's purely personal attitude and outlook upon life, governing all decisions arising under the grant of discretionary powers. This legally uncontrollable phase of all public action on the part of one set of public officials can be checked and balanced only by the same kind of manifestations of the personal equation on the part of another set of functionaries of the public service. Failing this method of control there is left as the *ultima ratio* only the judgment of the more or less indeterminable body of citizenry which in turn is the result of an indefinable mixture of individual and personal peculiarities of desires, prejudices and passions. This leaves as the sole remedy extra-legal action, the same kind of action which is supposed to have been responsible for the *de facto* establishment of the political organization of the body politic and for the original *de facto* formulation of the fundamental norms of the constitution. But since the human equation must thus be accepted as implied in all attempts at rationalization of human relations, the dependence on the part of the State upon extra-legal sanctions conditioned by the admission of this legally uncontrollable human element in all State actions, can in no way be said to militate against the juristic conception of the State and Sovereignty.

CHAPTER IX

Denial of Sovereignty by Duguit, Laski, and Others

Social Solidarity and Group Allegiance. Another phase of the criticism of the juristic conception of the State has taken the form of the out-and-out denial of the personality of the State as a clumsy fiction and of Sovereignty as an unnecessary and dangerous myth. An excellent review of this movement is given by Harold J. Laski in "A Note on M. Duguit," published in the Harvard Law Review, November, 1917, where he writes in part as follows: "We seem on the threshold of a new epoch in the history of the State. The movement towards what is vaguely called the socialization of law is in fact symptomatic of a far wider and deeper political synthesis. Distinguished thinkers all over the world do not hesitate to examine with scant respect the traditional institutions of modern government. Psychologists like Mr. Graham Wallas, sociologists like M. Émile Durkheim, political theorists like Mr. Ernest Barker, are all of them insistent that the traditional defense of parliamentary government has broken down. The great society has outgrown the mould to which the nineteenth century would have fashioned it. The life of the community can no longer be contained in, or satisfied with, its political achievement. It is not so much the general content of our ideals that has been called into question. Rather has a grave doubt been raised whether the present mechanism of politics is likely to take us much further in the direction of their attainment." [1]

The pioneer in this movement is Léon Duguit, a Frenchman. The essence and results of Duguit's ideas could hardly be summarized more briefly and at the same time more precisely than in the words of Laski: "Roughly speaking, M. Duguit denies at once the personality and sovereignty of the state. He denies the personality of the state on the ground that it is a clumsy fiction. The only realities are human beings; and to attribute their personality to what is a mere bracket connecting the collective action of some few of their number seems to him an antiquated anthropomorphism that imperils the scientific basis of law. He denies sovereignty of the state because it seems to him to imply the existence of rights where he sees only the existence of duties. Starting from the obvious fact of social interdependence, he insists that the only justifiable legal theory of the state is one that should enable it to satisfy the clear necessities of the time. But since that accomplishment depends upon the effort of each one of us, all that we possess is not the right to obtain the satisfaction of our individual wills, but the duty to contribute our energetic co-operation to the satisfaction of the social need." [2]

As Laski's survey of the movement shows, the tendency to question the character of the State as an organ clothed with the supreme legal power to control the actions of the individual for the benefit of the whole group is by no

[1] Laski, A Note on M. Duguit (Harvard Law Review, November 1917, p. 187). A statement almost identical with this is found in Laski's introduction to Duguit's Law in the Modern State....tr. by Frida and Harold Laski, New York, 1919, p. x, where Laski gives references to the works of Wallas, Durkheim, Barker, and others.

[2] Laski, A Note on M. Duguit, p. 189.

means confined to France. In fact, Laski himself is the able exponent of the doctrine of group allegiance or political pluralism which seemingly aims to dis-establish the theory of the Sovereignty of the State by substituting for the present allegiance of the citizen to the State the adhesion or loyalty of the individual to some of the economic, social or other groups existing within and forming the body politic.[3]

These tendencies are based on the assumption that the results of theoretical political thought, such as the juristic conception of the State and Sovereignty, can no longer be brought to embrace certain apparently new phenomena of the fast developing and expanding practical activities of State life. Such phenomena may be found in the constantly growing demands for the regulation of industrial enterprises, in the universally recognized need for increased attention by the State to the ethical and social aspect of the group, and finally, in the threatening reality of struggling personality against harrassing interference with the life of the individual or the association as members of the State. But underlying the whole problem is the apparent inability to realize that the shortcomings attributed to the State and the supposedly erroneous conception of its rights and powers are in reality either the results of the failure of the governing agents to interpret

[3] Concerning Laski's writings on this subject see Bibliography. In this connection reference should be made to the fact that this emphasizing of the group life in the State has its origin in Giercke's theory concerning the Genossenschaft. Giercke introduced the view that the medieval concept of the Genossenschaft (Corporation, Societas) as *persona ficta*, was wrong, that to the contrary all corporations within the State are real persons with a life and a will transcending those of the sum total of their members. (Gierke. Political Theories of the Middle Ages....tr. by Maitland....1913). On this subject see also Willoughby, Fundamental Concepts of Public Law, p. 40 ff. Laski, while accepting the autonomous position of the corporations

correctly the needs of the group, or the consequence of an excess of governmental activity to the detriment of the individual member of the political society. It is not the State which has become forgetful of the general good of the group and the individual welfare of the citizen as far as this is achieved by the former, but the governors who legislate, execute and apply laws made for the special benefit of particular interests and to the detriment of others. What is needed is not a lowering of the legal authority of the State, but a strengthening and widening of the State's legal methods of control over the agents entrusted with the realization of the aims for which the group is organized. A more detailed consideration of Duguit's theories from this point of view will tend to prove the correctness of this interpretation.

Confusion of State and Government. To Duguit the conception of national Sovereignty or legal supremacy as an essential attribute of the State is just a plain and discarded myth. But what he thus denies to the State he seems to grant to the governing agencies or ruling individuals to a degree infinitely more dangerous than legal Sovereignty of the nation-State, to which he is so violently opposed. Concluding an analysis of the political and economic situation in France and in general as the under-

within the State, denies the superiority of the State over these groups within its sphere of activity or territory. In his latest work (The Grammar of Politics, 1925) Laski, like Duguit in his Droit Constitutionnel, 1923, proceeds to the denial of State Sovereignty in favor of the primacy of international law as the expression and manifestation of the supremacy of the superior interests of the Society of Nations. On the subject of group allegiance or political pluralism see F. W. Coker: Pluralistic Theories and the Attack upon State Sovereignty, constituting chapter III of the memorial volume contributed by students of the late W. A. Dunning, edited by C. E. Merriam; also W. Y. Elliott: Sovereign State or Sovereign Group (The American Political Science Review, vol. XIX, 1925, pp. 476-499).

lying force driving Duguit in the direction in which he moves, Laski writes: "In such an atmosphere, it is against this theory of the sovereign State that M. Duguit's work has been a magistral protest. His earliest book [L'État ....1901-03] remains its fullest exposition. In a treatise on constitutional law [Traité de droit constitutionnel.... 1911] ....he has traced its ramifications through the field best fitted to display its import. In three lectures at the École des Hautes Études Sociales [Le droit social, Le droit individuel, et L'état....1908] he has effectively summarized their bearing. The volume here translated [Law in the Modern State....1919] relates his theories to the whole course of modern public law, and is, perhaps, the best summary of their general result."[4] It is from this work that the following quotations are taken. Having given an historical outline of that fiction called national Sovereignty Duguit says:

"With some rare exceptions there was no class or party in the nineteenth century which did not accept national sovereignty as a religious dogma. It is indeed true that those who drew up the preamble of the Charter of 1814 affirmed the permanence of the monarchical principle and divine right; but that was a platonic concession to the wishes of Louis XVIII and it deceived no one; 1830 was the re-statement of the principle of national sovereignty. The doctrinaires of course criticised with vigorous penetration the fruitless artificiality of this conception of sovereignty; but its criticism had no practical result..... The Revolution of 1848 was made in the name of national sovereignty; and it was again in its name that the monarchies of Europe were overthrown. Universal and equal suffrage and the majority principle which is illogically

[4] Law in the Modern State....Preface, p. xvi.

deduced from it took deep root in France. From France it has spread over the whole world.[5]

"There has come a change. With the beginning of a new century the clear and decisive question is defined by asking what reality this principle of sovereignty possesses. It has been ably and boldly criticised. August Comte tilted in his powerful fashion against it. 'In the thirty years of my philosophical career,' he wrote, 'I have always pictured the sovereignty of the people as an oppressive mystery, and equality has seemed to me an ignoble illusion.' Since then the dogma has declined, and no one has more powerfully attacked it than the theorists of the *Action française* and those of revolutionary syndicalism.[6]

"The former do not deny the existence of public power. They urge, however, that it does not belong and cannot belong to the nation, which from its nature, is incapable of self-government. It can belong, as French tradition has long taught, only to a national king whose dynastic interest is at one with the interests of the country. From the positivist standpoint, Deherme has arrived at the same conclusion, though he substitutes a dictator for kingship. The syndicalists attacked the very principle of political power and, drawing their inspiration from Proudhon, urge that economic organization ought to replace and is replacing the idea of political organization...." [7]

For a detailed discussion of these doctrines Duguit refers to Guy-Grand.[8] He agrees with them only in so far as they deny national Sovereignty. But his own denial of national Sovereignty is based on the fact that the term

[5] *Ibid.*, pp. 16-17.
[6] *Ibid.*, p. 17.
[7] *Ibid.*, pp. 17-18.
[8] Le Procès de la démocratie....1909.

Nation as used in the political or legal sense, i. e. Society organized as the State, is not identical with the term as used in the social and ethnographic meaning. Thus he writes:

"There are innumerable social and political facts with which the Revolutionary theory of sovereignty is incompatible. I will take only the most striking which group themselves under two heads: (1) National sovereignty implies an exact correspondence which in fact is often non-existent between state and nation; (2) national sovereignty is by definition one and indivisible; it implies the suppression in the national territory of all groups exercising independent control.....

"That there is often no correspondence between state and nation can be immediately shown. Sometimes the same government controls several distinct groups each of which is undeniably a nation. Often enough these nations are even rivals and remain united only by their common subordination to superior power.... Nobody doubts that there is an English people, but it is not less certain that the Irish people are no part of it. The United Kingdom is of course a state; but it is not a single nation organized as a state. What we have is rather a government imposed on three distinct nations.[9]

"Again the power of government is exercised over a large number of individuals who, without forming an autonomous nation, do not favor part of that nation of which the state is principally composed. Every government exerts power over men who are not subject to it but merely found on its territory. The inhabitants of colonies are

[9] Duguit, Law in the Modern State, pp. 18-19.

subject to the mother state without being members of its constituent nation....."[10]

According to Duguit such facts make impossible the theory of national Sovereignty and have profoundly shaken the faith of statesmen and jurists in the Sovereignty of the State.[11] But what does Duguit offer in place of this discarded Sovereignty of the State? Nothing more or less than "the idea of public service" the elements of which he defines as follows:

"These [elements] are in fact already clear. They consist essentially in the existence of a legal obligation of the rulers in a given country, that is to say of those in fact who possess power, to ensure without interruption the fulfilment of certain tasks...."[12]

But who are these rulers; what is the nature of the obligation which is imposed upon them; what is the purpose of this obligation?

[10] *Ibid.*, p. 19.

[11] Duguit refers to Esmein as the only French jurist who "remains unmoved amidst the ruins of an ancient system" (*Ibid.*, p. 35). Esmein holds that "the State is the legal personification of the Nation....it is the subject and basis of public authority. The basis of public law is found in yielding to a sovereignty outside and above those who exercise it at any given moment an abstract and an ideal subject which personifies the whole nation. This person is the State. Its essential quality is its relation to sovereignty" (Droit constitutionnel, 5 and 6 ed. pp. 1-2). It should be added that in his defense of the juristic conception of the State Esmein finds excellent company in his compatriot and colleague R. C. Malberg whose recent work on the theory of the State (Contribution à le théorie générale de l'État, 1920) is based upon the concept of the juristic personality of the State and of Sovereignty as the essential characteristic of the body politic viewed as a legal person. See especially chapters of the Contribution dealing with the theory of the personality of the State (vol. I, pp. 11-67), and with the theory of popular and national Sovereignty (vol. II, pp. 152-193), also quotations from Malberg given in chapter XII, notes 5-6.

[12] Duguit, Law in the Modern State, p. 39.

First: "Who are the rulers? From what has already been said it is clear that in actual fact they are not the representatives of a sovereign and collective person called the nation. We no longer believe in the dogma of national sovereignty any more than in the dogma of divine right. The rulers are those who actually have the power of compulsion in their hands. Why and how do they possess it? These are questions which can receive no general answer. The fact of possession is the product of historical, economic, and social forces which vary in each country. Governmental organization cannot evade the categories of space and time. But all these elements, however important, are not of primary significance. The broad fact remains that in any given country there is a man or a group of men who can impose on others material constraint. It therefore follows that power is not a right but simply an ability to act. Right could be assumed when we believe that it came from a divine investiture or from a delegation of a collective personality and as such had a will superior to individual wills. To-day, however, these religious and metaphysical beliefs have passed away. The power of governmental control is no longer a right but simply a power to act." [13]

Second: What is the nature of the obligation imposed upon the ruler? Duguit's answer is this: "If the right of government has passed away, its obligations remain. In every age the mass of men felt that the holders of power could not legitimately exact obedience save in return for certain services and to the degree in which they perform those services. Times without number social classes have lost political power because they no longer rendered the social services which were the conditions of its existence. This feeling, long dimly felt by men, is to-day everywhere

[13] *Ibid.*, p. 40.

understood. That is why we do not merely affirm it but rather search eagerly to determine, as the essential problem of the modern state, the legal basis of these obligations. It would of course be easy to postulate a moral obligation based on one or other of current ethical systems. But no ethical system escapes criticism. Any ethical solution is the result of a personal impression, what it is fashionable to call an intuition, and not from a rigidly scientific affirmation. The modern mind demands for its social problem clear solutions based upon the seasoned observation of facts. It is not moreover a merely moral obligation that is imposed on government; it is also a legal obligation which can be given a scientifically organised sanction. When this scientific sanction exists we have the right to assume that the legal obligation of government is a reality....[14]

"....Since, at bottom, law is the creation of the human conscience it may be asserted that legal obligations are imposed on government simply because we are to-day determined that it shall not be otherwise. We may assert that fact because, as I shall show, we have spontaneously organised the institutions of the modern state simply to give a positive sanction to these obligations. Sociological jurisprudence has sought to determine the facts from which they are derived. Personally, it seems to me clear that its real basis is social interdependence. That attitude doubtless is open to serious objections; the fact still remains that it is a conception which provides a suggestive solution to our problem. It is important, moreover, that this idea of governmental obligation should be so widespread. Law and the rule of law are derived from the profound belief of the mass of men, that a given rule is

[14] *Ibid.*, pp. 40-41.

imperative, that a certain task must be accomplished. Law, in brief, is above everything the psychological creation of men determined by their material, intellectual, and moral needs. That does not affirm the existence of a social conscience distinct from individual consciences. So to affirm would be to enter upon a dangerous metaphysical adventure.

"If it is certain that governmental power has very diverse causes, material, economic, moral, religious, it seems equally clear that it can only maintain itself in any durable fashion through the belief of its subjects that their rulers perform their functions. This is true whether the belief is accurate or not. Superstition and ignorance may well make a government seem profitable to its subjects when in fact it is not. There has been a vital element of political power and public law which, it is worth noting, is quite outside the realm of the social contract. That theory suggested that men united by an agreement and gave up their natural isolation; so was born a sovereignty and collective will which constitutes government. The fact, on the contrary, is that we have to start with a social group. The distinction between rulers and subjects is spontaneously produced and the former's power is imposed on the latter to a degree which varies with the belief and its utility.

"There exists then an intimate relation between the possession of power and the obligation to perform certain services. It is a relation so clearly understood and desired as in itself to provide a sufficient basis for the legal duties of government. All over the world to-day every ruler, emperor, king, president, minister, parliament, holds power not for his own but for his subjects' advantage, and the idea is so widespread that every statesman repeats it to nauseation even while in fact he tried to obtain the greatest advantage from his position."[15]

Third: What is the purpose of this obligation? In other words, what is the object of government? The answer to this question is found already in the preceding quotation. The object of government is on the one hand the performance of certain functions necessitated by the basic fact of social interdependence as the justification of the body politic; and on the other hand the performance of these functions in such a fashion that the people, believing in their successful performance will not depose those in power in favor of others more successful in the judgment of the public.

But what are the methods by which the rulers may convince the people of their success as governors? In other words, what are the functions of the rulers and what are the means by which they can impose their will upon the governed? To answer this question we must begin with the concept of law, public and private as defined by Duguit:

"The basis of public law is....no longer command but organization. Public law has become objective just as private law is no longer based on individual right or the autonomy of a private will, but upon the idea of a social function imposed on every person. So government has in its turn a social function to fulfil.

"The consequences of this conception are immediately clear. Their detailed examination will show that the formula I have suggested is not merely a theory but actually an induction from the facts. It follows that if governmental action is not the exercise of a right to power

[15] *Ibid.*, pp. 42-44.

it has no special character. What quality it possesses, what effect it produces are derived from the end it has in view. This in its turn determines the nature of law. In all the imperialist system[s] law is essentially the manifestation of sovereignty. It is above all a command formulated by the sovereign and so imposed upon his subjects. That is no longer the case. Law is simply the formulation of a rule, the product of a group of social facts which government believes necessary, as a rule, under the pressure of public opinion, in order to give itself the greatest possible strength. Most laws are in reality passed to organize and operate public utilities. Law is thus above all a law of public service.

"The importance of this theory is obvious. It sets the method in which law to-day functions in a clear light. Government is legally obliged to ensure the operation of public utilities. It issues for this purpose general rules called laws. Their character is derived from the end government sets before itself. The rulers themselves are inviolable. The private citizen can only use a public service as the law provides and government can do nothing which may prevent its legal operation. That is to say that public utilities are institutions of objective law." [16]

"Public utilities have thus an objective character. The law which governs them is only the recognition and operation of a general governmental duty. All administrative acts have a similar character because they serve a similar and public end. In these formulæ the new system may be resumed. Government and its officials are no longer the masters of men imposing the sovereign will on their subjects. They are no longer the organs of a corporate person issuing its commands. They are simply the managers of

[16] *Ibid.*, pp. 49-50.

the nation's business. It should thus be clear, contrary to the usual notion, that the growth and extension of state activity does not necessarily increase the government's power. Their business increases, their duties expand; but their right of control is extinct because no one any longer believes in it." [17]

But while their right of control thus is said to be extinct, their obligation to control is apparently very much alive and control as here used implies also method of coercion. Proof of this is found in Duguit's approving reference to the following interesting demonstrations of such control and coercion. "In October 1910, the French railway strike, partial and shortlived as it was, showed clearly that railroad transport has every element of a public service." As is well known, the French President ordered the army engineers to take the place of the strikers and thus prevented disorganization of public life. "Similarly, the English miners' strike of 1912, by the disaster that it might well have entailed, showed that the time is coming when the coal miners must be organized as a public service, and when Mr. Asquith persuaded parliament to impose upon the coal owners the duty of establishing a minimum wage he took the first step towards their transformation into a public service." [18]

Duguit's confusion of State and Government is exhibited most clearly in that part of the book here referred to, in which he deals with the State's obligation arising under civil claims for damages inflicted upon a third party by the functionaries of the State. Speaking of the office of the French President Duguit writes:

"....In the political system inaugurated by the constitutions of 1791 and 1848 the chief of the state was

[17] *Ibid.*, p. 51.
[18] *Ibid.*, p. 48.

clothed with executive power in its original sense and was thus the true incarnation of one constitutional element of sovereignty. He had a representative character in the field of the executive such as parliament exercised in the field of legislation. His acts were thus the direct emanation of national sovereignty and, like parliamentary acts, beyond the scope of administrative law.

"Undoubtedly those who constructed the constitution of 1875 had the same conception in mind. This is clearly shown by the Septennial Law, 'which confided for seven years executive power to Marshal MacMahon.' Successive presidents were to have the same character as he. Like him, they were to have that part of sovereignty we call the executive power. They were to be representative of the nation and so beyond the reach of law.

"Since 1875 the president has progressively lost his character. Little by little he has ceased to be a representative of national sovereignty. He has been simply an administrative agent, a high agent, indeed, of the administrative hierarchy, but still no more than an agent. As a result, all his acts can, as a matter of principle, be attacked on the ground of their *ultra vires* character. This change is not connected with the disappearance of the imperialist notion of sovereignty. That notion might have remained unbroken even though the character of the presidency had changed. The two evolutions are parallel but independent. The principle cause of the change is to be found in the origin of the office. From the fact that he is elected by parliament it has been concluded that the latter alone is a representative organ concentrating in itself all sovereignty, and it has been suggested that since it makes the president, he can be only an administrative agent. It is in this way that the transformation of his office has been harmonized with the general evolution of public law that no act of his is beyond the reach of justice."[19]

Reaction to Bureaucracy and Over-Centralization. Confusion of the concepts and functions of State and Government, however, is not a sufficient cause for the extent to which Duguit is ready to go in the direction of disqualifying the State. The explanation of Duguit's extreme position in this respect will have to be sought in the fact that he developed his theories in the atmosphere of the French economic, political and social struggles of the last two decades before the war. As Laski points out, the revolt against *étatisme* in France started with the ordeal of the Dreyfus case which caused a tremendous wave of public distrust in the Government. The disturbances of this case were followed by the struggle which finally secured the separation of Church and State, and by the tremendous labors involved in the formulation of the Law of Associations. On top of these problems came the contest of the great body of civil service employees for a more democratic organization. Virtually still under the heirarchical system which Napoleon I had created, the whole army of the *fonctionnaires* was actually and directly at the mercy of the *ministre,* and politician. The law of Associations prepared the way for trade-unionism of the government employees. And finally French labor in the syndicalist movement set up a system of economic and social units within the State.

It was in the midst of this atmosphere that Duguit came to deny the idea of the personality of the State, and of Sovereignty as its attribute and essence. In the place of the State, i. e. the political group viewed as a supreme lawgiver, he posits the social group in which all individuals

[19] *Ibid.*, pp. 175-176.

co-ordinate their activity for the purpose of achieving the groups' social aims. In the place of Sovereignty he posits social solidarity as the sole force binding the individual. The functionaries of the group have no rights, but only duties, namely to insure the realization of the social aims of the totality of the individuals, i. e. the group. In the final paragraphs of "The Law and the State," a peroration of the various German concepts of the State as an organ and system of force and power, Duguit asserts that: "Those who govern have power only for the purpose of fulfilling their obligations and only to the extent that they fulfill them. The State is not a power that commands. The State is a differentiated society in which the strongest must employ the force at their disposal to assure the accomplishment of certain services for the benefit of all...."

"In the doctrine of social solidarity....," he continues, "we find a complete refutation of the ancient conception of the State; and we can also say, a refutation of the German conception. Thus, where we saw....a power which has the right of issuing commands, and which can compel by force obedience to its orders, we may now see only a group of men obliged by the social principle (la règle sociale) to use their activity and their strength in the service of all." [20]

Concluding the study here cited Duguit quotes with approval part of the introduction of a book written by him in 1912, which is important in so far as it shows the full extent to which he is willing to go to illustrate his doctrine by practical application: This is what he wrote in 1912 and quotes in 1917: "The principle underlying the whole system of modern public law may be summarized in the following proposition: Those who in fact hold the power

[20] Duguit, The Law and the State (Harvard Law Review, vol. XXXI, November, 1917, pp. 183-184).

do not have a subjective right of public power; but they are under the obligation to employ their power to organize public service, to assure and control its development. None of their acts are of binding force or of political value, except when they tend toward this end. Public law is no longer a collection of principles to be applied to subjects of rights of different kinds—the one superior, the other subordinate; the one having the right to command, the other the right to obey. All wills are individual wills; all are equivalent in value; there is no hierarchy of wills. All wills are equal if one considers the subject only. Their value can be determined only by the end which they pursue. The will of those who govern has no force as such; it has value and force only to the extent that it makes for the organization and the functioning of a public service. Thus, the notion of public service comes to replace that of sovereignty. The State is no longer a sovereign power which commands; it is a group of individuals having in their control forces which they must employ to create and to manage public service. The notion of public service becomes, therefore, the fundamental notion of modern public law." [21] "These lines," Duguit adds, "written before the war, are truer to-day than ever."

The extreme views contained in these lines may, of course, always be regarded as useful or effective where and when an ill balanced governmental machine fails to further the common interests of the people as crystallized in the ideals and demands of the numerous economic and social

[21] *Ibid.*, pp. 184-185.

groups, or where too much government tends to subordinate these common interests to the demands and orders of a stratified body of governing officials. For it is in situations like these that such theories as the denial of Sovereignty or the denial of the binding force of the action of government serve their purpose of swinging the pendulum back from its extreme oscillations to a normal movement. One cannot escape the thought that the replacement of the legal supremacy of the State by the notion of social solidarity or group allegiance, if intended as more than a legitimate protest against existing evils of governments, would lead to a disintegration of modern civilization similar in effect to the dissolution experienced by society from the thirteenth to the seventeenth centuries. It would restore the autocratic rule of a democratized guild system aggravated by the competition of the equally autocratic capitalist brotherhood, both claiming to be the champion exponents of social solidarity and as such the legitimate recipients of the allegiance of *hoi polloi*. In regard to the immediate and very practical effects of Duguit's or Laski's denial of Sovereignty in favor of social solidarity and group allegiance, it is difficult to perceive how anything like an appearance of social and political order could have resulted from the chaos of central Europe in the fall of 1918, if their ideas had been applied by the builders of the new States then created and by the framers of the new constitutions then in the making.

As a matter of fact, one feels inclined to think that it was considerations of this kind which finally induced both Duguit and Laski to find a substitute for their discarded

State Sovereignty in the doctrine of the supremacy of international law as a theory holding out hope for the establishment of legal norms for the conduct of the nation-State. But the supremacy of international law presupposes the primacy or Sovereignty of an organization, a *civitas maxima,* or League of Nation, conceived as a kind of super-State. It would thus presuppose the return to a state of affairs very much like the situation of the Roman Empire under the nominal Imperium of the Greek or German Emperors, i. e. a theoretical universal Empire without the actual power to realize its pretensions.[22]

[22] This aspect of the doctrines of Duguit and Laski will be considered in chapter X and following, dealing with the theories of the Viennese or Austrian School.

CHAPTER X

The State and the Civitas Maxima According to the Austrian School

Kelsen's Concept of the State as a Juristic Person. The concepts of State and Sovereignty discussed in the preceding chapters are based upon the tacit assumption or expressed assertion of the primacy of State over international law. The doctrine of the supremacy of the law of the land over that of the society of nations is founded on either the denial of the legal character of international law, or the theory that though both municipal and international law are law in the true or positive sense, the latter is so only by sufferance (Selbstverpflichtung or Anerkennung) of the individual State. According to the Viennese or Austrian School whatever primacy there exists in the sphere of law, belongs to the law of the Society of Nations. Private, constitutional and international law are not different kinds of law, but varying forms of the one law, i. e. the supreme will of the *civitas maxima,* the universal State, which alone is sovereign and from whose Sovereignty the individual State derives its competency. The State as conceived to-day, i. e. the Nation-State, as Laski calls it, is not the source, but the manifestation of law. It does not exist antecedant to the law, but it is co-existent or identical with the law. It forms part of the law.

The chief representatives of this school are probably Alfred Verdross,[1] Fritz Sander,[2] Walter Henrich,[3] Josef

[1] See Bibliography.

[2] *Ibid.*

[3] *Ibid.*

Kunz,[4] and best known of all, Hans Kelsen. The latter's doctrine of the State and Sovereignty, to be discussed in some detail below, was developed in three stages, identified with his three chief works: (1) Hauptprobleme der Staatsrechtslehre....1911, re-issued in a considerably modified form in 1923; (2) Das Problem der Souveränität ....1920; and (3) Der soziologische und der juristische Staatsbegriff.....1922.[5] In the first edition of the Hauptprobleme Kelsen undertook to develop the science of law on a purely speculative basis, holding that the science of law or jurisprudence must be constructed by purely juristic concepts free from the ingredients of moral or political considerations. It was on the basis of this philosophical construction of the concept of law that Kelsen came to reject as formally erroneous the conventional theory of the dual character of the State viewed from the social aspect as the source and subject of power, and from the juristic point of view as the creator and protector of law. "The aim of the Hauptprobleme," he writes in the 1923 edition of this work, "and that of all my other works, is a pure jurisprudence as a theory of positive law. I have....endeavored to defend the purity of science [of law] or its equivalent—the independence of law as an object of scientific cognition—on the one hand against the claims of the so-called sociological point of view....and on the other hand against the doctrine of natural law....It is the main object of the Hauptprobleme to establish the autonomous character of law (die Eigengesetzlichkeit des Rechts) with regard to nature or any social reality determined after the manner of nature. It is for this reason that the Hauptprobleme start with the fundamental contrast between

[4] *Ibid.*

[5] For other writings of Kelsen bearing on the same subject see Bibliography.

Sollen and Sein, a contrast so to say first discovered by Kant in his attempt to establish the independence of practical as differentiated from the theoretical reason ...." [6] The realization of the difficulties confronting the juristic conception in the admixture of ethical and political principles, though already manifested in the Hauptprobleme of 1911, became more apparent in his later works, as for instance in an article published in 1913.[7] As a result of the rejection of the theory of natural law Kelson also turns against the dualism of subjective and objective, and of private and public law, as remnants of the Roman "Advokatenjustiz." [8] Subjective law is merely a derivative from objective law. Public and private law are two forms of one uniform system of legal order, the existence of which was anticipated in the Hauptprobleme and was finally accepted by Kelsen under the influence of Verdross,[9] and Kunz [10] whose writings move in the same direction.

In the Hauptprobleme of 1911 Kelsen still struggled with a two-fold paradox. The State as the bearer and manifestation or personification of law was at the same time conceived as a juristic person and as such the subject of legal rights and duties. Being thus conceived as a juristic person and the subject of legal rights and duties Kelsen held that the State must be placed on an equal footing with other legal, or at least with physical persons.

[6] Hauptprobleme....1923, pp. V-VI.

[7] Zur Lehre vom öffentlichen Rechtsgeschäft (Archiv des öffentl. Rechts, vol. 31, p. 247 ff.).

[8] Hauptprobleme....1923, pp. vii-viii.

[9] Grundlagen und Grundlegungen des Völkerrechts (Zeitschrift für internat. Recht, vol. 29, p. 65 ff.); Die Einheit des Weltbildes....1923.

[10] Völkerrechtswissenschaft und reine Völkerlehre (Wiener wissenschaftliche Studien. N. F. vol. III, 1922). Other contemporaries accepting the unity of the legal order are Nelson (Die Rechtswissenschaft ohne Recht, 1917), Krabbe, Laski, Duguit, a. o. See below, notes 41-43).

Viewed as the essence and bearer of law, however, the State must as a binding authority be considered as superior to other persons. Kelsen attempted to solve the difficulty involved on the basis of the difference between juristic and other persons, or as he states it, between Person und Mensch. Thus the State acts as a superior binding authority not upon the (juristic) person, but upon man (Mensch), i. e. the physical person. However, the concept of the uniform system of the legal order demanded the abandonment of the dualism of this differentiation between juristic and physical person in their relation to the State. All human acts of commission and omission were seen by Kelsen as partaking of a legal relation and to form the content of legal norms (den Inhalt von Rechtsnormen). It is the sum total (Zusammenfassung) of these actions personified which makes or constitutes the juristic person.[11] According to Kelsen it is this definition of the concept of the juristic person which renders it possible to conceive "the State as a Rechtssubjekt, i. e. the subject of rights and duties and as being [at the same time] identical with the legal order." [12] It is this conclusion which in Kelsen's opinion obviates the need for the makeshift of the so-called self-restriction (Selbstverpflichtung) of the State, which has been resorted to by Jellinek and others to explain the principle of a voluntary submission by the State to its own legal norms.

The State Subject to International Law. The State of the Hauptprobleme is still the body politic claiming independence and Sovereignty in its own right, i. e. the State

[11] See in this connection Sander's criticism of Kelsen's theory: Rechtsdogmatic oder Theorie der Rechtserfahrung (Zeitschrift für öffentl. Recht, 1921, vol. 2, p. 511 ff.) and Kelsen's reply (*Ibid.*, 1922, vol. 3, p. 102 ff.).

[12] Hauptprobleme....1923, p. xix.

identified with its own legal system or order. The relation of this State to other States of its kind, and to the international order in general has been left untouched by the Hauptprobleme. As dealt with in Kelsen's "Staatsunrecht" the relations between the individual State and between a State and the international legal system are still treated on the basis of the dualistic concept of the fundamental difference between international and constitutional law. But in his second chief work dealing with the problem of Sovereignty and the theory of international law Kelsen abandons this dualism, squarely rejecting the theory of the Sovereignty of the State in the sense in which it has heretofore been defined, in favor of the doctrine of a State competency subordinate to international law as the only Sovereignty in existence. "My endeavor to establish a pure theory of jurisprudence, free especially from sociological and political elements....," Kelsen writes in the introduction to this work, "is in this study directed towards a problem which in the treatment received in the prevailing theory has proven itself particularly needy of reform.... Heretofore I have evaded the problem of Sovereignty....for the simple reason that a solution....is not possible without a fundamental examination of the theory of international law. For the answer to the question of the character of Sovereignty, and especially to the question of its significance (Wesentlichkeit) for the State conceived as a legal order, depends upon the relation of international law to the legal system of the State. It is the examination of this relation between the two legal systems which forms the principle object of this work, and the recognition of the necessary unity of the two systems is its important result." [13]

[13] Das Problem der Souveränität und die Theorie des Völkerrechts, p. iii.

By a juristic hypothesis Kelsen thus posits the *civitas maxima*, the Bundesstaat *par excellence* as the State unit from which all other bodies politic derive their competencies, much in the same manner in which this super-State was first conceived by Christian Wolff [14] in the middle of the eighteenth, and as it was re-stated by Kaltenborn [15] about the middle of the nineteenth century. To quote Kelsen's own words: "In the generally accepted theory the character and concept of international law presupposes the community of equal States. The concept of the co-existence of a multitude of commonwealths which, despite their difference in size, population and effective power, are equal from the point of view of law—and, though mutually restricted with regard to their spheres of competence, are united in a higher community,—is an eminently moral idea and one of the few really valuable and undeniable elements of our modern cultural consciousness. But this concept is possible only by means of a juristic hypothesis, to the effect that above the States, viewed as commonwealths, there exists a legal order which demarks the mutual competencies (Geltungsbereiche) of the individual States, preventing interference with the competency of the one by the other, or making it dependent on certain conditions equally binding upon all. This legal order regulates the mutual relations of the commonwealths by norms equally pertaining to all; in the formulation of specific legal relations it excludes in principle any higher legal valuation of the one over the other; as a universal order it lifts the individual legal orders, personified as legal subjects, from their isolation and from their superlative valuation as Sovereignties, and thereafter unites them as part- or member-systems into a whole, i. e. a

[14] Grundsätze des Natur- und Völckerrechts....1754.

[15] Kritik des Völkerrechts....1847.

community [of States]. But international law can do this only if its primacy over the legal order of the State is accepted, i. e. if. . . . it is conceived as a legal system standing 'above' the State. . . ." [16]

Though Kelsen admits that this primacy can be established only by a juristic hypothesis, he takes exception to the charge that he attempts to construct his system of positive law "abstractly," i. e. "somehow from preconceived ideas." To explain the apparent contradiction he differentiates between the validity and the content of a legal norm. "The individual legal rule of a judgment, of an administrative act, or of a legal transaction, has its origin in the general norm of the law, the law in turn in the still more general norm of the constitution, and the constitution, finally, in a generally supreme principle representing the logical source which, as a juristic hypothesis, establishes the constituent authority (die als juristische Hypothese die verfassunggebende Authorität einsetzt)." But Kelsen is conscious of the fact that, "though the constitution derives its legal validity from the preconceived original principle (aus der vorausgesetzten Ursprungsnorm), it receives its content from the emperical willing act of the constituent authority; just as the law derives its validity from the constitution, but its content from the fact of its enactment as legislation (aus dem Faktum des Gesetzgebungsbeschlusses), and as the judgment receives its validity from the law but its content from the fact of the willing of the judicial act (aus dem Faktum des richterlichen Willensaktes). . . ." [17]

State and Law in the Universal Legal Order. Having thus asserted the supremacy of the *civitas maxima* over

[16] Das Problem der Souveränität und die Theorie des Völkerrechts, pp. 204-205.

[17] *Ibid.*, pp. v-vi.

the State, and that of international law as the legal order of the *civitas maxima* over the legal order of the member commonwealths, Kelsen proceeds to solve the remaining problem of the nature of the State, i. e. the problem of the relation of law and the State in the position thus assigned to the individual body politic in the universal legal order. This he attempts to do in his third main work treating of the sociological and the juristic concept of the State. As shown above, Kelsen rejects the dualism of the physical and juristic person (of Mensch and Person) with regard to the legal order personified as State. It is not man as a biological or psychological being who is the subject of legal rights or duties, but the juristic person conceived as the sum total of man's actions in relation to the legal system represented by and called State. Applying this concept to the State, itself viewed as a person, Kelsen writes: "In traditional constitutional law—man in the multitude forming the Staatsvolk, together with (neben), the Staatsgebiet and the Staatsgewalt, constitutes a so-called element of the State. But as in the pure science of jurisprudence man is not to be considered as a psycho-biological object, placed in opposition to the legal order or outside of the system of law...., and as the place of 'man' is taken by human action as the content of legal norms, thus also the other element of the State, i. e. its territory must be divested of its natural-geographical reality....and, transposed into the sphere of law, must, together with the Staatsvolk, be reduced to a common denominator (Nenner). It must be conceived as the local sphere of validity of the legal norms constituting the political order (der die staatliche Ordnung bildenden Rechtsnormen)" [18] Under this construction also the Staatsge-

[18] Hauptprobleme....1923, pp. xx-xxi. This theory has been worked out in great detail by Walter Henrich in his essays: Theorie des Staatsgebietes, 1922; *and* Das Sollen als Grundlage der Rechtswissenschaft (Zeitschrift für öffentl. Recht, 1921, vol. 2, p. 131 ff.).

walt, i. e. Sovereignty in the conventional sense, is no longer a reality but a legal relation or condition. As stated by Kelsen: "It is self-evident that, considered from this uniform aspect, Staats-'Gewalt' constitutes nothing but either the binding validity of the legal order, the legal order itself, or a special content of this order such as the commission of acts of compulsion (die von ihr statuierten Zwangsakte). Sovereignty does not constitute a kind of natural reality...."[19]

Kelsen is, of course, well aware that his considerations, limited as they are to juristic conceptions and their functional relations, do not comprehend the reality of so-called social facts. The conception of the State as a legal order, i. e. as an ideal system of valid legal norms, and its transposition into the sphere of the intellect, does by no means eliminate "the fact that there is, in the system of cause and effect, i. e. in the system of nature, something which corresponds to this ideal system of validity. Different as the legal norm as a specific content or meaning (Sinngehalt) is from the psychological act by which it is produced, there nevertheless remains the fact that only such norms can be conceived as valid, which are effective, i. e. borne by motivating concepts or acts of willing." This fact is as Kelsen admits "the root of the age-old question of the relation of might and right, which, though from their definition they are exclusive of each other, nevertheless are somehow related."[20] It is in this fact that Kelsen sees also the heart of the difficult problem of the positivist character of the law, the solution of which, "as far as such

[19] Hauptprobleme....1923, p. xxi.
[20] *Ibid.*

solution has any prospect of success," he is attempting in his third chief work cited.[21]

Kelsen's doctrine of the primacy of international law is not only diametrically opposed to the theory of those who hold that international law is not law at all, or that it is law only to the extent to which it is Staatsrecht,[22] i. e. exterior municipal law (äusseres Staatsrecht) as Hegel [23] calls it. It is also at variance with the theory of those who admit the independent legal character of both international and municipal law, but who attempt to establish some kind of relation between the two by the device of the voluntary obligation of the State (Selbstverpflichtung) or that of the recognition by the State of certain norms of international law (Anerkennungstheorie). Conceding that "logically the dualistic construction of the relation of international and municipal law is not impossible," [24] Kelsen insists that "the theory of international law must conceive both international and municipal law as two synchronous legal systems from a uniform juristic aspect comprising both legal orders." [25] Nor will Kelsen tolerate the attempt to solve the problem of the relation of international and municipal law by the confusion of the

[21] In this connection see also: Das Verhältnis von Staat und Recht im Lichte der Erkenntniskritik (Zeitschrift für öffentl. Recht, 1921, vol. 2, p. 453 ff.), which as Kelsen states in the introductory sentence constitutes in essence the closing chapter of "Der soziologische und der juristische Staatsbegriff."

[22] Treitschke, Politik. Vorlesungen hersg. von Cornicius. 2. ed. 1899, vol. I, p. 35 (Cited Kelsen, Probl. der Souveränität, p. 154 ff.); Philip Zorn, Die deutschen Staatsverträge (Zeitschrift für die gesamte Staatswissenschaft, vol. 36, 1880, p. 1 ff., cited *ibid.;* and Albert Zorn, Grundzüge des Völkerrechts, 2, ed., 1903 (cited *ibid.*).

[23] Hegel, Grundlinien der Philosophie des Rechts, oder Naturrecht und Staatswissenschaft im Grundrisse. 3 Aufl. 1854, p. 416 ff. (cited *ibid.*)

[24] Problem der Souveränität...., p. 150.

[25] *Ibid.*

dualistic and monistic constructions. As pointed out by Kelsen, both Triepel and Heilborn, for instance, accept the independent character of the two legal orders. "The theoretical researches of the preceding sections," Triepel writes in his Völkerrecht und Landrecht, "lead to the conception of international law and municipal law as two different legal orders. They constitute two complexes of legal norms, each originating from another source." [26] In the same work, however, Triepel states that "all law (Recht) is somehow connected (hängt unter sich eng zusammen), no part permits of a strict severance (Absonderung). It may be, however, that the connection between the legal branches within the whole realm of the legal system of the State are more apparent than the often rather delicate threads running from municipal to international law. But though these threads may be delicate, they are nevertheless firm. For that reason it is possible but not advisable to ignore them." [27] International law, according to Triepel, is the sum total of the legal norms constituting the common will of the individual States, conceived as a legal order completely independent from the particular wills of the individual States. [28] But this international common will stands above the States by whose individual will it is established and as such it is legally binding upon them. International law stands as a power above the State, just as municipal law stands above the citizen, for "a legal norm, which does not stand as a power (Macht) above the subjects to whom it is directed," Triepel can not conceive. Heilborn, like Triepel, starts from

[26] Triepel, Völkerrecht und Landesrecht....1899, p. 156.

[27] *Ibid.*, p. 2.

[28] *Ibid.*, p. 61, p. 76 ff. Triepel's concept of international law as the common will of the compacting States is based on Binding's detailed elaboration of this theory. See the latter's Zum Werden und Leben der Staaten....1920, p. 191 ff.

the dualistic construction, positing the original independence of international and municipal law. Like Triepel he deduces the binding character of certain international legal norms from the recognition (Anerkennung) [29] of these norms by the individual State. "International law is deducible not indirectly, but directly and immediately from the will of those States upon which it is binding (massgebend). The fact that an international legal norm is valid for all other States is meaningless to the one State which has not recognized that norm." [30] But while the State is held to be bound by the international legal norms to which it has given its recognition, international law on the other hand asserts a certain degree of superiority over the State by its own recognition of particular spheres of competence (Sovereignty) exercised by the State. According to Heilborn "international law recognizes the State as the subject of law, it concedes to the organs of the State a particular legal position and it determines the effectiveness of their acts in relation to other States." [31] But "just as private law concedes to man a legal power over certain interests (Güter), so international law concedes such legal power to the State," for "the individual interests of the particular State are as valid (massgebend) for international law as the individual interest of man is for private law." [32]

[29] The Anerkennungstheorie of Triepel and Heilborn differs, according to Kelsen, only in name from the Selbstverpflichtungstheorie of Bergbohm (Staatsverträge und Gesetze als Quellen des Völkerrechts ....1877, p. 19 ff.), and of Jellinek (Die rechtliche Natur der Staatsverträge....1880, p. 7 ff.). See Kelsen, Probleme der Souveränität, p. 138.

[30] Heilborn, Grundbegriffe des Völkerrechts (Handbuch des Völkerrechts, hrsg. von Stier-Somlo, bd. I., abt. I., 1912, p. 33.

[31] *Ibid.*, p. 89.

[32] *Ibid.*, p. 106.

In the opinion of Kelsen, all these attempts to posit, on the one hand, the independence of both international and municipal law, and to establish on the other hand some kind of interrelation between the two by way of the Selbstverpflichtung of the State or by the mutual Anerkennung of each other's competencies or norms, are due to the common error of viewing the State as a reality, as a Naturding, as a kind of man, rather than as an order or system. Thus the behavior of this personified State, like that of man, is conceived as the object of two different legal orders, that of its 'own' legal State order, and that of the international legal system.[33] But according to Kelsen the State does not *possess* a legal order peculiar to itself, it *constitutes* such an order.[34] Hence the admission of the binding quality of the international legal system over the State is equivalent to the admission of the relation of unity between the supposedly different legal orders of State and international law. To let Kelsen speak for himself: "Triepel and Heilborn do not doubt that international law obligates the State. If international law is, as both

[33] Problem der Souveränität...., p. 143.

[34] It is on the basis of this distinction between the State's possession of and the identity with its own legal order that Kelsen rejects the idea of the Staatsunrecht, i. e. the ability of the State to commit a legal wrong and to assume the legal responsibility for such a wrong. It is not the State but the organs of the State who commit the wrong. Kelsen defines an international legal duty of the State as follows: "Men, obligated by the legal order of the State to a certain course of action and who as such are organs of the State, shall as such, i. e. within their constitutional authorization, act in a definite manner determined by international law...." Thus any human action incompatible with international legal obligation does not constitute an act of an organ of the State, and as such is non existant. The so-called "Unrecht of the State is always only the condition, never the content of the (legal) will and action of a State." But according to Kelsen "This does not preclude the possibility of an international legal wrong, it only rejects the construction that such a wrong is that of the Staatsperson" (Problem der Souveränität p. 143 ff.).

concede, law, and if, as both concede, it is not a mere part (Bestandteil) of municipal law—what else can it be than a legal system standing above the municipal legal order (Landesrechtsordnung)...., i. e. a system which, because it obligates the same subject, must stand in a relation of unity with the Landesrechtsordnung? Could the municipal legal order obligate the community if the communal order were not subordinate to the legal order of the State, delegated by it and forming a system of norms within the municipal legal order (eine Teilordnung der staatlichen Rechtsordnung bildendes Normensystem); [in short] if the community, as a legal subject, were anything but the personification of the communal order?" [35]

Primacy of International Law in the Realm of Facts. Though Kelsen thus posits the unity of the legal order and clearly as far as he is concerned subordinates municipal to international law within this uniform order, he nevertheless concedes, as pointed out, that "logically the dualistic construction of the relation of international and municipal law is not impossible." [36] It is on this point that mostly all the other members of the so-called Viennese School differ. In a lecture "On the Theoretical Basis of the Law of Nations" delivered before the British Grotius Society, Professor Kunz of Vienna, takes Kelsen to task for this concession. Referring to the hypothesis of the primacy of international law as "the only right one" he said in part: "Kelsen gives its delineation, and there can be no doubt that he himself inclines to this construction; but he professes that from the *theoretical* standpoint, both the mon-

[35] *Ibid.*, pp. 139-142.
[36] *Ibid.*, p. 150.

istic constructions are equally possible...."[37] Kunz considers this "to be the weak point of Kelsen's construction." The reason for Kelsen's error is to be found in the latter's "conception of the relations between rules and facts in the world of law," and "in his conception of a 'hypothesis'." According to Kunz "Kelsen is, no doubt, a strong partisan of positivism in jurisprudence; but he does not refer enough to the *positive empirical* rules of International Law, and he often states that the choice of the fundamental hypothesis is, juridically speaking, arbitrary." But Kunz holds that this "is not true" and that it "means a total misunderstanding of the nature of the *scientific* hypothesis." Conceding that "it is a great merit of Kelsen to have introduced into jurisprudence the method of the hypothesis," Kunz points out that "not every hypothesis is a scientific one," the inference, of course, being that Kelsen's hypothesis is not scientific. "Science," Professor Kunz stated, "does not permit a vague hypothesis which has its origin only in a wild imagination, but a hypothesis alone which is able to guarantee, according to the status of our present cognition, the best possible connection of all that is given by experience. The juridical hypothesis is presupposed by the cognition of the jurisprudence as a basis towards the unity of cognition, and has to conform to the material that is given by experience, as Kelsen himself says now in one of his last works [Rechtswissenschaft und Recht]."

Applied to the problem here discussed this means that according to Professor Kunz "the decisive point as regards

[37] By the phrase "both the monistic constructions" he means the primacy of municipal over international law and that of international over municipal law, while Kelsen, in the passage quoted, refers to the dualistic construction, that is the theory of a mutual independence of both legal orders (Problem der Souveränität, p. 137 ff.).

the two constructions of International Law—primacy of the law of the land and primacy of the law of the nations—is, from our *theoretical* standpoint, only the following one: Which of the two hypotheses is able to guarantee the connection of the material of all the positive rules of International Law, given by experience, into one system (in itself and at the same time into one system with all that is law, i. e., also with the law of the land) in the best possible way, according to the present state of knowledge?" It means further, that "if the hypothesis of the primacy of the law of the land is not able to guarantee this connection it must, from a purely *theoretical* point of view, be abandoned." And Professor Kunz is certain, "that the hypothesis of the primacy of the law of the land is not able to do so." For "according to this hypothesis, International Law must be considered as having its basis in the Constitution of the single States." Admitting that "a large part of the rules of International Law could be considered as deriving their force from the Constitution as a superior law" he insists that this cannot be true of all of them. "Take for instance the very common case of the change of a Constitution by law or by revolution. If International Law has its force only in the Constitution, it logically must cease to have this force if the superior law, the Constitution, itself loses its force. But there exists without doubt a positive rule of International Law that the State remains the same; in spite of the change of Constitution or Government, that International Law remains binding also upon this State under the new Constitution or upon the new Government." And "how would you explain the binding force of common International Law upon new States, which have not yet been recognized by other States?" Answering his own question he asserts that: "Only our hypothesis, our theory alone, of the primacy of

International Law can give the construction in *one* system of law. According to this theory, International Law is, of course, the superior law to the law of the land. But this superiority, this sovereignty, of International Law is not a political but a theoretical one; it is not, as Austin said, a sovereignty of the *political* superior to a *political* inferior (for we are always within the system of *law* and not of (*politics*), but the sovereignty of a superior *law* to an inferior *law*."

Nevertheless even Professor Kunz cannot entirely ignore the political or practical aspect of the question. He insists that "certainly this construction is also the most desirable from the standpoint of the *politics* of International Law, for it is only under this hypothesis that a development of a true Law of Nations will be possible." But he admits this "desirability....would prove nothing at all for our *theoretical* construction, for it would be in this case the theoretical construction of some International Law of the future as we desire it, a construction of an International Law *de lege ferenda*," while what he has been speaking of is a "construction of the positive Law of Nations *de lege lata*." [38]

Professor Kunz suggests "it can be proved that the hypothesis of the primacy of International Law alone is able to create a systematic connection of all the present positive rules of International Law." He is "glad to state that our theory of the Vienna School is gaining ground, especially in Italy." He informed his hearers that "you will find hardly a theoretical page in the *Rivista di diritto internazionale* where the books of Kelsen, etc., are not cited; and one of the greatest living international lawyers,

[38] For preceding quotations from Professor Kunz's article see Transactions of the Grotius Society, vol. 10, 1925, pp. 138-140.

Dionisio Anzilotti, has altered the second edition of his *Corso di Diritto Internazionale,* especially under the influence of Kelsen's writings." But Professor Kunz concludes with the warning that though "Science and theory are the same things," we must nevertheless "not overrate the importance of a theory. Theories are essentially only a useful way of research, as said Henri Poincaré; there is no such thing and can be no such thing, as a theory which will last forever. For precisely because the hypothesis in our case has to conform to the positive rules of International Law, it is clear that, with a complete change of International Law, the scientific hypothesis and theory of the system of International Law must change too. . . ." [39]

Professor Kunz might have added that the theory of the primacy of international law has been acclaimed in principle, though as it seems independently of the Viennese School, by such contemporary authorities as Salvioli,[40] Krabbe,[41] Laski,[42] and Duguit.[43] The endorsement of the doctrine by men such as these certainly must mean a great deal for all those who hope that the construction of international law *de lege ferenda* will some day be realized as a construction of the positive law of nations *de lege lata.* But their acclamation of the theory of the primacy of in-

[39] *Ibid.*, pp. 140-141.

[40] Rivista di diritto internazionale, XIV, 1921-22, Serie III, p. 20 ff., p. 34 ff.

[41] The modern Idea of the State, chapter X.

[42] Grammar of Politics, p. 65 ff., 238 ff., 662 ff.

[43] Traité de droit constitutionnel, 1921, 2. ed., vol. 1, pp. 99-110, 550-565. Duguit holds that the economic, moral, and juridical norms of international law are applicable not to the fictitious legal personalities called States, but to governments as their agents and to individuals constituting their citizenry. But Duguit does not believe that a *civitas maxima* or super-State is needed for the enforcement of these norms. He is convinced that the faith of the people in these norms will secure for them recognition and compliance.

ternational law does not establish the fact of such primacy. Nor does their denial of the Sovereignty of the State on this or on any other ground disestablish that Sovereignty as long as the premises upon which their denial is founded are matters of opinion and assertion rather than demonstrable facts. And since the Sovereignty of the nation-State is thus only denied but not disestablished, the juristic conception of the State based upon or positing that Sovereignty must be recognized as a factor to be reckoned with. What will become of that conception when the theory of the primacy of international law becomes a reality, and to what extent it will be able to survive by adaptation and modification, is a question to be considered in the concluding chapter. In the meantime we shall proceed to the examination of the German idea of the State as a juristic person, an idea which follows somewhat of a middle course between Willoughby's doctrine positing the legal omnipotence of the sovereign State, and the Viennese School's assertion of the Sovereignty of the *civitas maxima* as the legal superior of the nation-State.

CHAPTER XI

German Conception of Sovereignty Without Independence

Definition of the State as a Legal Person. In the preceding chapters we have dealt with the juristic conception of the State both from the point of view of the primacy of municipal over international law and from that of the supremacy of international law over the law of the land. In the present chapter we have to consider a concept of the State as a juristic person and of Sovereignty based upon the assumption that Statehood and Sovereignty are independent of the status of the State from the point of view of international law, or rather, that Statehood and Sovereignty are not conditional upon independence as an essential attribute of the State.

German theories of the State have recently been reviewed by Professor Anschütz in a study on German constitutional law, published in volume IV of Holtzendorff's Enzyklopädie der Rechtswissenschaft.[1] In this study Anschütz comes to the conclusion that "of all the theories of the State it is the theory of the personality of the State which to-day has found the widest acceptance." According to Anschütz, this general acceptance "corresponds to its intrinsic worth, for it is the theory of the personality of the State which alone on a purely juristic basis offers a

[1] Deutsches Staatsrecht (Holtzendorff's Enzyklopädie der Rechtswissenschaft....IV. 1914). A comprehensive examination in English of the evolution of German constitutional theory is found in Duguit's "The Law and the State. French and German Doctrines," (Harvard Law Review, vol. XXXI, November, 1917).

non-contradictory explanation of the concept of the State in agreement with modern political thinking." [2]

Analyzing the criteria of the non-contradictory character of the juristic conception of the State as a legal personality, Anschütz enumerates certain requirements demanded by modern political thinking of any satisfactory definition of the State and met by no other doctrine than that of the juristic personality of the State. These requirements are:

1. A unity of the State transcending the changing relations of the governors and governed.

2. The quality of the State as a unity endowed with power and will, capable of action, the subject of rights and duties.

3. The character of the State as a social unit consisting of human beings, or the nature of the State as a commonwealth; the nature of the State's will as a common will (Gemeinwille); the nature of Sovereignty (Staatsgewalt) as corporate competence or power.

4. The inclusion in the State corporation of the rulers, one or many, i. e. the inclusion of those exercising the corporate power in the State corporation in such a way that the ruler is not placed outside or above the corporation, but is included as its principal servant (erster Diener), in other words, in such a way that the king in ruling does not maintain his own, but someone else's, namely the State's, law.[3]

The juristic conception of the State is presented as the generally valid theory of the time also in Georg Meyer's Lehrbuch des deutschen Staatsrechts, of which the seventh edition, prepared by Anschütz, appeared in the early

[2] Anschütz, Deutsches Staatsrecht, p. 11.

[3] *Ibid.*

part of 1919.[4] As stated by Anschütz, this edition, though published in 1919, is based on the constitutional jurisprudence of the Monarchy. According to Meyer-Anschütz, the State, from the juristic point of view, is called a person, i. e. a Rechtssubjekt of public law. The right to rule its subjects belongs to the State as a commonwealth, not to the ruler, for the ruler is merely an organ of the State. Attention is called, however, to the fact that in the older version of the doctrine the right to rule was vested not in the State, but in the ruler as his personal Herrschergewalt and that this version had its supporters even at the end of the nineteenth century as for instance in Jellinek. Of the theory of the legal personality of the State it is said that "in modern constitutional jurisprudence it may be considered as generally valid for the juristic conception of the State."[5]

In his recent treatise on German and Prussian constitutional law Professor Hatschek accepts the juristic conception of the State, viewed as a legal personality endowed with a legal will, also for the constitutional jurisprudence of the Republic. The State, Hatschek admits, may be considered from a double aspect, i. e. from the point of view of social science and from that of jurisprudence. Rejecting the doctrine of the legal personality of the State as dangerous from the sociological aspect, he asserts the necessity of its acceptance from the point of view of jurisprudence. Considered from the sociological aspect the State is not a reality, but merely a function of Society. Viewed socially the State is nothing but a passing or rotation of human actions. These actions are, to be sure, of

[4] Referred to as Meyer-Anschütz.

[5] Meyer-Anschütz, p. 15.

a particular kind: they are directed towards the realization of specific aims, called the aims of the State, such as security of law, welfare, power. But he warns that we must realize that these aims do not exist as realities outside of ourselves. For we, and only we ourselves, create these aims in order to conceive this rotation of human action as having sense or meaning. To ignore this warning would, in Hatschek's opinion, "render us only too apt to consider the State as unity of will, as a collective personality" and this, in turn, "would lead to a dangerous apotheosis of the State." From the juristic point of view, however, the concept of the unity of will of the State, i. e. the concept of the legal personality of the State, is, according to Hatschek, not likely to serve as a basis for the glorification of the State for the reason that this concept, "introduced by us as an auxiliary construction, is our own creature" and as such "a fiction which we must accept for the better understanding of our legal order." [6]

Sovereignty: Staatsgewalt. Considered as a juristic person the State is endowed with a legal will like any other physical or legal person. This legal will the State possesses and exercises, for instance, in its fiscal activities. But in addition to this legal will which the State has in common with other legal persons, it has, as Anschütz points out, another will (Willensmacht) peculiar to itself, which is called Staatsgewalt, with the synonyms Staatshoheit and *Imperium*. As the terms Staatshoheit and Imperium suggest, the Staatsgewalt, peculiar to the State, is the sovereign will or the Sovereignty of the State.

Staatsgewalt Anschütz defines as "the competence (Gewalt) exclusively belonging to the State, or ruling

[6] Hatschek, Deutsches und preussisches Staatsrecht....1922, I., pp. 3-4.

land and people," which means that "the State's competence is supreme in its sphere, that its command has precedence over the commands of all other subordinate powers of the land, that its will breaks all resistance." [7]

According to German constitutional jurisprudence the Staatsgewalt is indivisible and irresistible. We cannot consider a personality in its component parts without destroying its unity. A division of the Staatsgewalt would result in the division of the State into as many new States, each with its own Staatsgewalt.[8] The irresistibility of the Staatsgewalt as an essential characteristic is, according to Anschütz, included in the definition of the term as the supreme competence or power of social coercion.[9]

In his discussion of the juristic conception of the State and Sovereignty in German republican jurisprudence, Professor Hatschek writes: "The State is a territorial corporation (Gebietskörperschaft) endowed with supreme Herrschermacht (Souveränetät).[10] Of the Herrschermacht or Souveränetät, called by Anschütz Staatsgewalt, Professor Hatschek says: "Souveränetät is merely a logical concept of relation, such as above, below, right or left ....It only means that the State within the sphere of its legal order does not recognize a superior lawgiver above itself." [11] Giving as the essential characteristics of the State viewed as a juristic person those of territory and population, Hatschek concludes that "to this must be

[7] Anschütz, pp. 17-18.

[8] His definition of the Staatsgewalt in the relation between National and component units in the Federal State will be considered below.

[9] Anschütz, Deutsches Staatsrecht, p. 18.

[10] Hatschek, I. p. 4. The spelling of the term Souveränetät varies with the German authorities here cited. Hatschek and Meyer spell it Souveränität, Anschütz Souveränetät. For the sake of uniformity one spelling has been followed in text and quotations.

[11] *Ibid.*

added Souveränetät in the sense described above, which includes the right of self-organization."[12]

From the preceding definition it seems to appear that the German term Staatsgewalt, or Herrschermacht as used by Hatschek, implies something more than Sovereignty as legal supremacy, or the will of the State expressed as law. There seems to be implied in it a connotation of political power or force which the term Sovereignty, in the sense used heretofore, does not so readily suggest. This difference, however, is only apparent. The fact is that the German word Staatsgewalt expresses the material aspect of the legal supremacy of the State, while the term Sovereignty in the sense of legal superiority expresses the formal aspect of this supremacy. But on the formal side the political power or force implied in the term Staatsgewalt connotes an attribute of the State as a subject of law exercising the Staatsgewalt exclusively in the form of legal action. On the other hand, the term Sovereignty as legal supremacy must imply on the material side the political power or force necessary to make legal superiority a reality.

Staatsgewalt as Distinguished from Souveränetät. Professor Anschütz considers the question whether independence (Unabhängigkeit) is an essential quality of the Staatsgewalt. Independence he defines as a quality of the State or Staatsgewalt as viewed from the aspect of international relations. The State is independent when it is not permanently subject to the command or restriction of another State. Thus the question whether independence is an essential attribute of the Staatsgewalt is, according to Anschütz, "identical with the other question, whether Sovereignty (Souveränetät) belongs to the characteristics

[12] *Ibid.*

without which a State no longer remains a State." In answer to this question Anschütz states that under Laband's influence German constitutional doctrine has come to hold that Souveränetät is not an essential attribute of the Staatsgewalt.[13] Accordingly the term Staatsgewalt is applied in German jurisprudence to denote the supremacy of the State in the sphere of constitutional law, covering the activities of the State within the sphere and reach of its own territory. The term Souveränetät is used to describe the independence (Unabhängigkeit) of the State in its relation to other States, i. e., in international relations and law.

The practice of German jurisprudence of distinguishing between the use of the terms Staatsgewalt and Souveränetät as here described has its basis in the historical development of the German States. It was the result of two conflicting tendencies within the Holy Roman Empire of the German Nation. These conflicting tendencies may be described as the effort on the part of the Empire or Emperor of subordinating under the National dominion the political units of the realm, and of the attempt of the political units of the Empire to escape from the dominion of the Empire or the Suzerainty of the Emperor. Not being able to reduce the princes of the Empire to permanent submission, the Emperor never succeeded in establishing the Sovereignty of the National realm. On the contrary, the princes succeeded in securing international recognition for their territories as States of international standing in the Treaty of Muenster of 1648 and finally in bringing about the dissolution of the shadowy Empire itself in 1806. The fact that in consequence of the successful termination of their primary and major struggle against the Sovereignty of the Emperor, the princes found them-

[13] Anschütz, Deutsches Staatsrecht, p. 24.

selves also in the possession of the supreme ruling power (Herrschermacht or Herrschergewalt) in the relation with their subjects was incidental rather than fundamental.

To the German rulers of the political units of the Empire the important aspect of Sovereignty was that of independence in the relation to Emperor and fellow rulers and it was this meaning of the term which has remained uppermost in its use. "Sovereignty (Souveränetät) is therefore independence of the State from powers which are above or outside of it."[14] The supremacy of the ruler over his own subjects, i. e. Sovereignty in the constitutional sense, came to be known as Herrschergewalt or Herrschermacht, i. e. competency to rule or ruling power. With the gradual encroachment of the supremacy of the State as the commonwealth or Nation over that of the personal ruler, the term Herrschergewalt or Herrschermacht was replaced by the term Staatsgewalt in the meaning of Sovereignty of the State in the sphere of constitutional law and activity.

The use of the term Staatsgewalt or Herrschermacht, in the sense of Sovereignty in constitutional law, and that of Souveränetät as independence is, however, by no means the universal practice of German writers. As a matter of fact, the absence of uniformity in the employment of technical terms and the variety of such terms for the same concept are a source of great difficulty in the study of German political philosophy and jurisprudence.[15] Nevertheless, the necessity of giving serious consideration to the difference of meaning of the terms Staatsgewalt and Souveränetät, as used by Anschütz, will appear from the fact that the

[14] *Ibid.*, p. 23.

[15] For the details of such inconsistency and of the use of synonyms see chapter III of the author's Principles of Constitutional Jurisprudence of the German National Republic.

German Republican Constitution altogether avoids the use of the term Souveränetät as Sovereignty in the constitutional sense, employing the term Staatsgewalt in its stead.

Statehood and Staatsgewalt without Independence. An additional reason justifying the preceding reference to the distinction in the use of the terms Staatsgewalt and Sovereignty is to be found in the fact that the historical premises for this distinction, though considerably modified, are still sufficiently active to force attention to Anschütz's particular usage of the terms in question. While it is true that the German States have finally sacrificed their position of independence in favor of National unity in the form of a federal Empire or Republic, the advocates of the States rights doctrine still insist upon Statehood and upon Staatsgewalt as qualities or attributes of the Länder within the limitations of the federal Constitution.

Historically the claim to Statehood for the German Länder is based upon the fact that with the formal dissolution of the Empire in 1806 their independence was formally recognized in international law and was maintained even in the establishment of the German Federation of 1815. The claim was kept alive after the creation of the North German Confederation of 1866 on the assumption that this union was effected by a compact of the princes and as such was perpetuated in 1871 in the transformation of the Confederation into the Empire.[16] Prevailing opinion of German constitutional jurists has long since discarded the compact theory in favor of the juristic conception of the State positing the *de facto* establishment of the Norddeutsche Bund and the legal continuity of the

[16] See on this subject chapter II of the author's work referred to in preceding note.

Empire, recognizing the impossibility of attempting a legal justification of the origin of the State. Prevailing opinion has also decided in favor of the State character and Sovereignty of the Bundesstaat and as such of the North German Confederation of 1866 and the Empire of 1871. Nevertheless an important element of German authorities have persisted in the claim of Statehood and Staatsgewalt (Landesgewalt) for the German commonwealths.

At the time of the Revolution in 1918 a strong movement made itself felt in favor of the establishment of a republican National unitary State in which the former States should be reduced to mere administrative units.[17] The so-called first Preuss draft of the National Constitution attempted to realize this desire. However, pressure from the States forced a considerable modification of the program of Preuss and his followers and the Constitution as finally accepted by the National Assembly is referred to by the States righters in substantiation of the State character of the Länder and of a residue of Sovereignty (Landesgewalt) possessed by the Länder in their own right.

While the extreme view in favor of the unitary character of the Republican Reich is held by such authorities as Giese, Poetzsch, Wenzel, et aliis, the Statehood and Staatsgewalt of the Länder is defended by Stier-Somlo, Jellinek, Arndt, and others.[18]

In his discussion of the republican constitutions of the Reich and of the Länder, Jellinek concedes that the Länder have lost in importance in the same degree in which the

[17] See note 16.

[18] See Brunet, The New German Constitution....tr. by Gollomb.... p. 70; and for individual treatment of these authorities the author's work referred to in note 15.

Reich has gained. The Länder still have in principle the full power of legislation. But there is left in them hardly an important sphere for the exercise of this power. With the removal of the income tax from the activities of the Länder they are deprived of their most important medium of independence (Selbständigkeit) in their relation to the Reich. The Länder still possess in principle their own system of judicial procedure and administration. But the administration and conduct of foreign and military affairs has been taken over by the Reich. Their share in the financial administration is insignificant, that of the railroads and rivers has been taken over by the Reich. The Länder still possess territorial Sovereignty (Gebietshoheit), but by national constitutional amendment, and in some cases, an ordinary national law, their territorial status may be altered. The Länder still have the constitutive power, but the Reich prescribes for them the republican and parliamentary form of government and the fundamental principles for the State and municipal election laws. Nevertheless Jellinek concludes that the Länder are States. Though Sovereignty, in the international legal sense, is the most certain attribute of the State, it is not the decisive one. If it were, the Länder would not be States for they are not sovereign in this sense.

According to Jellinek the criterion of the State character of the Länder is to be found in the answer to the question as to what the Länder would do, or would have to do, in case the superior system of the National Republic were suddenly removed from them. Finding themselves deprived of their present authority (Macht), would they dissolve in anarchy and be forced to reorganize, as in revolution or in the case of the formation of a new State? If so, then they are not States, but provinces or Länder. Would they, on the other hand, without interruption continue to exist on the basis of their present constitution? If they would do so, then the "Landesgewalt" is not one coming to them by the grace of the Reich, and the Länder are States even under the Constitution of the Reich. Measured by this criterion, Jellinek holds, the Länder are States. The republican form of government, he points out, had been accepted by the States (with the exception of Gotha) before it was prescribed by the National Constitution. The Länder still participate in the formation of the national will through their representation in the Reichsrat. Though the Reichsrat cannot prevent the enactment of national law, it can essentially influence national legislation by the enforcement of a popular referendum in the case of a disagreement with the Reichstag.[19]

The theory of the State character of the German Länder as here expressed by Jellinek, is shared also by Anschütz. In his work on German constitutional law of the Monarchy Anschütz, as mentioned above, holds that Sovereignty in the international legal sense, i. e. independence, is not an essential attribute of the State. Anschütz insists that under Laband's influence German juristic opinion has rejected the doctrine still adhered to by such eminent authorities as Seydel and Zorn, that a body politic, in order to be a State must possess Unabhängigkeit. According to Anschütz the doctrine that the State must possess independence, first proclaimed by Bodin, is both impolitic and unhistoric, at least from the point of view of the constitutional development of the German States which, he points out, as members of the Holy Roman Empire, have been for a long period the sole carriers of the new idea of the modern State. After sixty years of formal and actual independ-

[19] Jellinek, Revolution und Reichsverfassung (Jahrbuch des öffentlichen Rechts, vol. IX, pp. 80-81).

ence, to which they had no historical claim, they once more became member States of the North German Confederation formed in 1866. But States they remained and the Staatsgewalt retained by them they possessed in their own right. Positing, as he does, the indivisibility of the Staatsgewalt he holds that in the new National Union of 1866 and of 1871, as in every Bundesstaat, indivisibility of the Staatsgewalt was not in question.[20] In the German Empire there was, according to Anschütz, only the Staatsgewalt of the States. The Empire possessed no Staatsgewalt above and aside from that of the Länder. It did not even share the Staatsgewalt of the States, but merely participated in the exercise of functions arising under the Sovereignties of the several States.[21]

In his commentary on the National Republican Constitution Anschütz accepts what he seems to consider as a dual, not divided, Staatsgewalt. Article 1, Section 2 and Article 5 of the Constitution of 1919 state respectively that "the Staatsgewalt emanates from the people" and "the Staatsgewalt is exercised in national affairs by the organs of the Reich in accordance with the National Constitution, in the affairs of the Länder by the organs of the Länder in accordance with the constitutions of the Länder." These provisions Anschütz interprets to the effect that the Staatsgewalt exercised by the National Government emanates from the German people, that exercised by the Länder emanates from the people of the Länder. Hence he follows that according to the National Republican Constitution the Länder are commonwealths subordinate to the Reich, but possessed of a Staatsgewalt in their own right, i. e. a

[20] See note 13.

[21] Deutsches Staatsrecht, p. 20.

Staatsgewalt which they have not received as a lien from the Reich, nor from anybody else. The Länder are therefore States under the Republic as well as under the Empire. "What elevates the State above the non-State and especially above the community," Anschütz writes, "is not Souveränetät (independence from the outside and from above), but the originality and the non-delegated character (Eigenständigkeit) of the Herrschergewalt.... According to the new as well as the old law, the German individual States, now called Länder, have not lost their Statehood by their adherence to the Reich...." [22]

[22] Anschütz, Verfassung des Deutschen Reichs vom 11. August 1919, p. 29.

CHAPTER XII

THE JURISTIC CONCEPTION OF THE STATE RESTATED

Object and Scope of Restatement. Concluding his analysis of Willoughby's conception of the doctrine Crane was of the opinion that though the theory in this particular version "has a legitimate sphere of validity and utility," it has "been carried far beyond any legitimate scope" and for this reason "needs a critical restatement." [1]

This opinion was based upon the assumption that the doctrine as expounded by Willoughby was not in agreement with the realities of political life within the State and with the actualties of the relations of the State to other States of its own pattern.

Vinogradoff's modification of the theory constitutes such a restatement from the point of view of the alleged incompatibility of the doctrine with the realities of the internal political and constitutional aspect. In the discussion of Vinogradoff's version the attempt has been made to show that the charge of the incompatibility of the juristic conception of the State with the actualities of politics is based upon a misunderstanding of the theory on the part of the critic rather than upon any disqualifying features of the doctrine itself. But it must be admitted that developments have taken place which lend added vigor to the criticism of the doctrine with regard to its tenability from the point of view of international law. Since 1918 the establishment of the League of Nations has given substance to the idea of the supremacy of international law over municipal law, an idea developed into an elaborate

[1] Crane, Discussion [of Willoughby's The Juristic Conception of the State] (The American Political Science Review, XII, 1918, p. 214).

doctrinal system by the Viennese or Austrian School and ably supported by such eminent authorities as Krabbe, Laski and others.[2] Since then a number of new States have been created, ostensibly on the basis of the juristic conception of the State as a sovereign and independent body politic, professing at the same time allegiance to the League of Nations. The treaties of peace were signed individually and avowedly in their own rights by a number of political entities nominally subject to the Sovereignty of Great Britain. Some of these units have actually established diplomatic representatives in foreign capitals. Ireland has assumed the official title of a Free State, though it is constrained to acknowledge the Sovereignty of the British Crown. In Germany a new National Constitution has been created which rests squarely upon the juristic conception of the State considered as a sovereign and independent body politic, but which nevertheless allows a number of apparently sincere jurists, statesmen and politicians to assert the State character and the possession of Staatshoheit or Staatsgewalt by the member commonwealths constituting the Reich. In the chapters dealing with Crane's, Laski's, Duguit's and Vinogradoff's criticism and modification of Willoughby's version of the juristic conception of the State the effort has been made to examine in a detached and purely judicial manner the facts involved. The same can be said of the presentation of the doctrine of the Viennese School, positing the primacy of international over municipal law. In each case the consequences have been indicated which the establishment of these facts must or would have upon either the original tenets of the doctrine or upon the modification offered by its critics. What remains to be done here is to correlate, as far as possible, facts and consequences into a uniform

[2] See chapter X, notes 40-43 and corresponding text.

and consistent restatement of the juristic concept of the State and Sovereignty or of their equivalents according to the new light in which we may have to view them. This being the object of the restatement, it fixes at the same time its scope inasmuch as a restatement is justified only to the extent to which the original doctrine is or may be affected by new facts or conditions demanding consideration and recognition.

Corporate Character of the State. The juristic conception of the State presupposes the existence of a politically organized group of individuals conceived as constituting an essential unity or body politic which it happens to call State.[3] It is this group of individuals, politically organized, which is regarded as a juristic person, much the same way in which for instance a private corporation is viewed as a person from the point of view of the law. As we ascribe to the private corporation a legal will, so, similarly, we recognize the State as having a legal will which, in this case, we choose to call Sovereignty, if for no other reason than for want of a more fitting term. But while in jurisprudence both the State and the private corporation are conceived as legal persons, each possessed of a legal will,

[3] The term State has been chosen instead of Nation, because the latter has not yet acquired a sufficiently uniform meaning suitable for a generally applicable definition. While the French and English use the term Nation as denoting the entire people forming the body politic, German authorities point out that the term Nation signifies something narrower than that. They use the term "Volks," "Staatsvolk," to identify the people constituting the State. Nation, they say, may mean only part of the people of the State. Switzerland, though a State, comprises three Nations (We should say nationalities). On the other hand, a people as a social unit may be a Nation (nationality) without being a State. Ireland, for instance, no doubt has always been a Nation (nationality) but not a State. (See in this connection: Willoughby, The Nature of the State, p. 9 ff.; and Fundamental Concepts of Public Law, p. 60.)

there are some vital differences distinguishing the two. The consideration of these differences will, more than anything else, bring into relief the essentials of the State viewed as a legal personality.

A private corporation may be described as an organization of individuals possessing certain well-defined mutual aims. The object of their organization is the realization of these aims. Prior to the chartering or incorporation of this organization, the legal rights and duties of the corporation are those of its individual members as natural legal persons. By the act of incorporation or by the grant of a legal charter the law recognizes the corporation itself as a legal entity or unit. It now deals no longer with the individual members but with the corporation as if it were a natural person. We say that the corporation has become a legal person or a person before the law.[4]

The will of the corporation as a legal person is expressed no longer by and through its individual members, but

[4] In the California Law Review, vol. XIII, March 1925, "E. O. E." discusses a California Court decision in Wenban Estate v. Hewlett. In this decision the court claimed to cast aside the legal fiction of independent corporate existence. Commenting on this phrase "E. O. E." denies the fictitious character of the concept of corporate existence. "To realize that this doctrine is not a legal fiction," he says, "one need only look at the purposes of incorporation. These are accomplished by obtaining, from the state, the privilege of acting, in regard to the corporate enterprise, in a special capacity, separate and distinct from the individual capacities of the members. From this separation result the right to sue in the common name, perpetual succession, limited liability, etc. The doctrine of separate corporate entity is therefore not a fiction, but a metaphorical method of describing the legal truth that the rights and liabilities of the corporation are to be kept separate and distinct from those of the individual shareholders. To say that this privilege is a fiction is simple a failure to understand its nature. As the United States Circuit Court [U. S. v. Milwaukee Refrigeration Transit Co.] said: 'A corporation, as expressive of legal rights and powers, is no more fictitious or intangible than a man's right to his own home or his own life'."

through the officers of the corporation. The officers are elected by the members of the corporation. They are legally bound to act for the corporation in accordance with the corporation's statutes or charter provisions formulated to express the fundamental principles upon which the share holders or members on the one hand, and the State on the other, wish to have the business of the corporation transacted. Thus the corporation, not its individual members, enters into legal relations with other legal persons. The corporation, not its individual members, is held principally liable by the law for the fulfilment of its legal obligations.

Before the law, the corporation as a legal person remains the same no matter how often its stock changes hands from one set of shareholders to another.

It is for eminently practical reasons that the corporation is considered as a person before the law. Now in much the same way politically organized society, called the State, is, for purely practical reasons, considered a legal person, and this personification of the State before the law is as real and tangible as that of the corporation.

As the corporation has been defined as an organization of individuals possessing certain mutual interests or aims, so the State is viewed as the political organization of a social group conscious of definite mutual interests and purposes. As the members of the corporation organize for the realization of the aims of its members, so the social group is found to form a body politic for the materialization of its national or group interests. As the corporation is merely the unitary aspect of its individual members, so the State is nothing but the uniform manifestation of a citizenry conscious and desirous of political cohesion. Thus the State is not a superstructure reared above the citizenry constituting the body politic. The State is the body politic, it is the Nation, using the term in its wider application.

As in the case of the corporation, for very practical reasons viewed as a legal person, the individual membership expresses its will through the officers of the corporation, so the citizenry of the Nation or State expresses its will as the will of the State through the governing agents of the State. As the officers of the corporation conduct the corporation's business in accordance with the charter or statutes, so the governing agents of the State transact the Nation's business in conformity with the established practice of constitutional convention or in obedience to the definite legal norms of a written constitution representing the ideas and principles by which the citizens forming the Nation or State wish to be governed.

Just as the corporation viewed as a legal person remains the same though its shareholders constantly change, so the State, considered as a person before the law, maintains its identity with the passing of one generation of its citizenry after another.

But here the analogy ends. For whereas the corporation becomes a person before the law by the granting of a charter by the State, i. e. by the act of incorporation under the laws of the State, the Nation is considered as possessing the character of a legal person by its own right, i. e. by the mere fact of its *de facto* political organization. Whereas the corporation thus assumes legal rights by the sanction of the superior law of the State, the Nation as the State is considered as possessing legal right as the supreme authority and the source of all law in the body politic. The State is considered as the supreme legal authority and as the source of all positive law in the body politic because there is within its sphere of will and action no other legal authority superior to itself in this respect.[5] By the same token we must insist that, whereas we ascribe to the corporation viewed as a legal person a legal origin in the act of incorporation under the laws of the State, we find it impossible to ascribe a legal origin to the State. The existence of the State is to be recognized subjectively by virtue of the manifestation of political organization of a particular social group, objectively the Statehood of this politically organized social group is attested to by the official or practical recognition on the part of other States.[6]

Whereas the corporation as a legal person has legal duties as a natural corollary to its legal rights by virtue and force of the superior law of the State, the Nation as the State can be said to have duties only as obligations assumed by virtue of its own legal will, i. e. in consequence of its own law. Such legal obligations accrue from the

[5] As well stated by Duguit's colleague and compatriot Malberg: "Le fondement de la notion de personnalité juridique est le même pour toutes les collectivités personnalisées que pour l'Etat. Ce qui fait d'un groupe ou d'un éstablissement une personne, c'est qu'il est constitué en un organisme doué d'une capacité propre de droits. Mais, entre l'État et les autres personnes juridiques, il estiste cette différence capitale que celles-ci, nées sous l'empire du droit étatique, prennent la source de leur organisation dans un acte juridique, et notamment peuvent la prendre dans un contrat formé entre les fondateurs du groupe: au contraire, à la base de l'État, il ne peut être question de contrat social, parce que, le droit n'existant que par l'État, ce contrat anté-étatique sérait dépourvu de valeur juridique...." (Malberg, Contribution à la théorie générale de l'État...., vol. I, p. 68).

[6] See also Malberg who concludes his discussion of this question as follows: "Du point de vue juridique, ce fait générateur de l'État consiste précisément en ceci qu'un groupe national se trouve constitué en une unité collective, en tant qu'à un moment donné il commence à être pourvu d'organes voulant et agissant pour son compte et en son nom. A partir du moment où elle est ainsi organisée d'une façon régulière et stable, la communauté nationale devient un État. Peu importe la voie par laquelle les individus qui lui servent d'organes, ont

State's activities as an employer of the agents conducting the Nation's business, or from its participation in the management of public utilities regulated by the State's own laws. But whereas the corporation is irrevocably held to the fulfilment of its legal duties by the superior law of the State, the Nation as the State is held to the observance of the legal obligations assumed by virtue of its own laws, by the obvious necessity of insuring the conduct of its affairs in such a way that the generally recognized mutual aims and interests of its citizenry are maintained and furthered rather than retarded and jeopardized.

There is within the State in addition to and above the State's own will or willingness to honor its own law no legal agency capable of ensuring such enforcement. Primarily then and in the last analysis we can speak of the obligations of the State only as receiving whatever binding force they have upon the State from considerations of an ethical or political, i. e. utilitarian character arising from the aims of society striving for and maintaining its political organization. As the source of positive law the State can, of course, modify or repeal a law entailing obligations too onerous or objectionable. But as a person before the law it cannot but honor these obligations as long as the law itself stands as its own sovereign and legal will. The very nature of the State viewed as a legal per-

acquis cette qualité ou capacité, et sont parvenus à établir que leur volonté vaille comme volonté unifiée de la collectivité....La conclusion qui se dégage de ces observations, c'est qu'il est vain de vouloir chercher un fondement juridique à l'État en dehors du fait de son organisation initiale. Sans doute l'État doit en réalité sa création à des volontés et à de l'activité humaines: Mais la question de savoir dans quelles conditions et en quelle forme ces volontés et activités se sont manifestées, demeure juridiquement indifférente. Le juriste n'a point, à se préoccuper des circonstances qui ont précédé l'apparition d'un État...." (Vol. I, p. 62-64).

son categorically demands the observance and enforcement by the State of whatever obligations arise under its own law for the simple reason that the refusal or failure of such observation and enforcement constitutes not merely a violation, but a repudiation of its own law and as such a contradiction and denial of its own expressed will. It surely involves no greater incongruity to demand that the State honor its own laws when partaking of activities subject to regulation by these laws, than to expect a parent to honor the rules of conduct established by him or her for the general benefit of the household to the extent to which they place restrictions upon the activities and conduct of the parent. Nor does it imply a greater degree of absurdity to assume that the State as the law giver can and will place obligations upon itself by its own law-making activity than to believe that a parent can and will in the exercise of parental authority, to the required extent, curtail his or her own freedom of action in the interest of their offspring. We are here dealing with an axiom or truism, not with a theory or hypothesis subject to reasoning and demonstration.

But while the State itself is thus held to the observation and enforcement of its own law by reason of a utilitarian nature, the obligations arising under the State's own law are legally binding upon the agents of the State charged with the execution of these laws and it is the State's business to insist upon and ensure the observation of these legal obligations by its agents in the manner provided by the laws in question. This phase of the problem, i. e. the differentiation between the utilitarian aspect of the obligations assumed by the State by its own law, and the legally binding nature of the State's law upon the magistracy of the State, has been considered in detail in connection with Laski's criticism and Vinogradoff's assertion that the State is the subject of legal rights and duties and therefore requires here only a passing reference.[7]

The State as the Source or Subject of Law. The preceding comparsion of the State with a private corporation and the subsequent differentiation between the two is based upon the assumption that the State is the source of all positive law enacted by its constitutional agencies for the conduct of its citizenry and its governing magistracy.

The attempts to posit as the source of law an agency or authority outside and above the State have so far not produced any convincing and demonstrable results. The reason is not far to seek. While the State, i. e. the Nation considered as society politically organized, can enact laws by a definite body or organ, and while it can enforce these laws upon its own magistracy and citizens, an agency or authority outside or above the State depends for the enforcement of its superior law entirely upon the hold which that law has upon the conscience of the leaders of the Nation.

Thus, divine law, for instance, and natural law as part of divine law, is certainly not enforcible upon a State. It can be considered as having any influence upon politically organized society only to the extent to which it inspires the individual with a sense of responsibility or awe. But even so there is no end of degrees to which the individuals of the national body may be subject to its sway, nor is there any standard or criterion by which the actual meaning and demands of that law can be established or demonstrated.

[7] See chapter VIII (The State as Subject of Legal Rights and duties).

No more is public opinion as the manifestation of Krabbe's sense of right qualified to be set up as the source of law or as the law itself of which the State is to be the expositor and executor. Public opinion is undoubtedly an important factor in the enactment of law by the State and must on occasion be relied upon to supply the corrective for a recalcitrant or unscrupulous legislature. But the best interests of the State very often demand that public opinion bow to the law as it stands or as it is made rather than that it dictate the enactment of legislation on subjects on which it is not at all or at least ill informed.

International law is, at the present day, not generally recognized as a law superior to and legally binding upon the nation-State. This is merely a statement of fact which is not to be interpreted to imply that some day international law may not be so recognized. But dealing with conditions as they prevail to-day, the Sovereignty of the State is a reality, not a myth, at least subjectively considered, that is from the point of view of the nation-State, and provided that by Sovereignty we understand something real and not something that can exist only in imagination. As brought out in an earlier chapter,[8] the concept of Sovereignty owes its origin to the struggle between the National monarch of the middle ages, especially in France, and the feudal lordlings for supremacy on the one hand, and for freedom from such supremacy on the other. It was a struggle aiming not at the establishment of a position of omnipotence, political or legal, but one of relative superiority or freedom from restraint.

The same is true with regard to the idea of national Sovereignty as it developed in revolutionary France and later in the United States of America and in present day

[8] Chapter I.

Germany. In revolutionary France it was not a question of how sovereign the French Nation was or was to be, but of who was or was to be the sovereign,—the King, as he had claimed up to that time, or the Nation, as the revolutionary National Convention or Assembly held it to be. In the United States the issue was, and in the German Reich it still is, whether the member States or the Federal Union is sovereign, i. e. whether the will, political or legal, of the States is to prevail over that of the National Union, or whether the will of the latter shall be valid over that of the States constituting the Union. Legal omnipotence, if we consent to the use of the term at all, must therefore be taken to signify not a state or position enabling the body politic to do anything and everything that the imagination might call for, but a condition qualifying the State to perform all those acts necessary for the realization of the best interests of the citizenry and of performing these acts without the legal interference on the part of any agency within the State or from without as matters stand at this time.

The State and the Civitas Maxima. It is true, there is a League of Nations based upon the acceptance by the members of the League of a so-called covenant by which these member States pledge themselves to the observation of certain conditions and to the performance of certain functions determined or determinable by certain specified premises. It is equally true that some of these conditions and functions partake of the character of servitudes. Nevertheless, it is a significant fact that at least most of the individual members of the League in theory as well as in practice claim the possession and exercise of Sovereignty both in the constitutional and international legal sense. There is no more emphatic and convincing proof of this claim than the insistance upon the unanimity of the vote in the League Council and the apparent eagerness for voting membership in that body; for this provision of the unanimity of the vote assures the individual voting member of a veto power equivalent to the assertion and exercise of its sovereign will and competence to prevent a decision contrary to its own interests of State. On the other hand the existence of servitudes is not *per se* a mark of the loss or absence of Sovereignty. As a matter of fact a common sense view of present day international relations compels the admission that there is to-day no State, however powerful and self sufficient in the matter of material resources and man power, which, from the point of view of its own best interest, can afford to ignore the legitimate interests of other States nor refuse to restrain its own freedom of action accordingly.

But the very fact that the right to the veto power implied in the unanimous vote of the League Council seems to be so jealously guarded by its voting members may be looked upon as an indication that there is danger ahead for the advocate of State Sovereignty and that the degree of vehemence in the defense of this veto right may well be held to signify the correct measure of this danger. While it is, of course, too early to form and express an opinion with regard to the probable outcome of the League of Nations as a practical experiment in the direction of the supremacy of international law over the so-called Sovereignty of the State, there can be but one kind of reaction to the fascinating idea of the Viennese School positing in theory the unity of all law with international law as the supreme Sovereignty from which all other political units derive their competence, political and legal.

According to the theory of the unity of law and the Sovereignty of the *civitas maxima,* the State of our present day conception would assume the same position with regard to the international Bundesstaat which the private corporation holds to-day in relation to the State. To-day there is such a thing as recognition of the State in international law. But such recognition does not constitute the creation of the State. In fact it pre-supposes the existence and effective functioning of a social or national group as a sovereign and independent body politic, i. e. as a State. International recognition signifies merely an objective acknowledgment of the subjectively existing Statehood of a particular political entity. Furthermore, this international recognition does not add in any degree to the Sovereignty claimed by the State in the constitutional sense. It merely affects the State's relations with other States. Not so under the doctrine of the unity of law and the supremacy of international law. As the private corporation receives its legal character and its statutes and by-laws receive their legally binding aspect by the act of incorporation under the law of the State, so the individual State would according to the doctrine of the primacy of international law. For according to this doctrine the State would enter into the full enjoyment of Statehood also in the constitutional legal sense only by the sanction of the *civitas maxima.* The degree of this dependence is of course problematical and varies in the different versions of the doctrines advanced by different members of the school. In general it may be said, however, that in the theory of Kelsen and his disciples the sovereign and independent State of to-day would be placed in more or less the same position in which the so-called free States of the British Empire and the Länder of the German Reich find themselves to-day. Compelled to acknowledge formally and actually the supremacy of the British Crown or King in Parliament and the Sovereignty of the German Reich, these subordinate units unquestionably maintain a certain degree of coercive power and control over their citizenry. They have freedom of will and action within a well defined sphere of activity. Some of the British Commonwealths have furthermore successfully assumed many of the outward characteristics of the independent State, such as the signing of peace treaties and the sending of diplomatic agents to foreign capitals.[9]

But how would such a development affect the doctrine of the juristic conception of the State and Sovereignty? As stated above the juristic conception of the State is not concerned with the historical origin of the State. It presupposes the existence of a politically organized group of individuals conceived as constituting an essential unity called State. Under the existing system of international relations we have many institutions claiming the character of a State as defined. In the vision of Kelsen and followers we would have only one institution entitled to that name. On this assumption the juristic conception of the State would remain exactly what it is to-day, with the one reservation that instead of applying to a number of bodies politic, it would be applicable to only one political organization embodying as subordinate units all the independent States of to-day.

We should still be compelled to admit that we cannot explain the creation or the existence of that super-State on any but a *de facto* basis. We should still have to define its laws as its sovereign will devoid of any authorization but its own instinct for self-preservation. We still should have to admit that the State, in this case the *civitas*

[9] The present day position and the aspirations of the commonwealths of the British Empire and the Länder of the German Reich for greater independence or a larger degree of "Sovereignty" will be discussed in the next chapter.

maxima would recognize no legal restrictions, within or outside itself, binding upon its own actions. We still should have to be satisfied with the morally or politically-binding principles embodied in the raison d'être of the super-State viewed as an institution best suited to realize the interest of society and individual.

Whether these morally or politically obligating principles would be more effective under the system of the primacy of the international super-State than they are under the present state of affairs is a matter of pure conjecture. All that can be said in this regard is that under present conditions it is considerations of practical politics in the treatment of the citizenry of the State which constitute the motive for the State to honor its own legal norms. Under the system of the *civitas maxima* it would be questions of practical politics with regard to the component State units, the conduct of which, however, is controlled in turn by their citizenry constituting each unit.

Little is to be said concerning the mere accidentals of the problem as these would depend chiefly upon the development of the more fundamental questions. Some of these accidentals are the mode and the extent of enforcement against the individual State of the legal norms of the *civitas maxima*. Clearly the answer to the question of such enforcement depends upon the more fundamental question of the degree and extent to which the super-State if in actual existence would be able to establish a legal supremacy over the individual State unit. Would it, for instance, be satisfied to regulate interstate economic and political relations? Or would it assume the right to control the individual State's relations to its own citizenry? In the first instance its mode of enforcing its will might be restricted to some actions employed to-day for the enforcement of a State's contractual or treaty obligation. In the second case the super-State would undoubtedly have to assume right of immediate action not against the State unit as such, but against the particular agency of the offending State whose actions constitute an infringement of its international obligation in the sphere of what we to-day call municipal or constitutional law.

So much for the prospects of the juristic conception of the State as applicable to the super-State under the theory of the primacy of international law. But what is to become of it with regard to the individual State units which are to constitute the imaginary or future super-State? The answer to this question is simple. It is patently not tenable with regard to the State unit considered as a member State of the sovereign *civitas maxima*. That is, it is not tenable with its present terminology. This brings us to the last consideration of the present study, i. e., the question whether any doctrine of State and Sovereignty and in particular the juristic conception of the State, is capable of a statement broad and simple enough to be generally applicable to any and all forms of State, or to what extent our present day terminology stands in the way of such a broadening and simplification. The answer to this question will be attempted in the next chapter.

CHAPTER XIII

General Applicability of the Jurisitic Conception of the State

Conflicting Terminology. The question of the general applicability of any theory of the State, and of the juristic conception of the State in particular, is considerably complicated by the apparent difficulty of deciding or determining in a given instance whether a certain body politic possesses all the earmarks of a full fledged State in the meaning of the theory or whether it does not possess them. It is not the difficulty of deciding whether the juristic conception of the State as endowed with Sovereignty applies to these particular political units, but whether they are recognized in international law as possessing statehood in the sense defined by the analytical jurist. This problem seems to be especially puzzling and troublesome in the case of the individual political units constituting the so-called Bundesstaat, such as the United States, the German Reich, the British Empire, the Union of Soviet Republics, and the former Austro-Hungarian Kaiserreich.

This phase of the problem has been considered to some extent by Willoughby in his Fundamental Concepts of Public Law in the chapter dealing with non-sovereign political bodies. Willoughby's examination of the problem leads him to the conclusion that "from the juristic standpoint, no fundamental distinction can be drawn between non-sovereign members of a federal State and their administrative units."[1] In other words member States of a Federal union are juristically speaking not independent States and as such can not claim Sovereignty in the inter-

[1] Willoughby, Fundamental Concepts of Public Law, p. 269.

national legal sense. But as Willoughby rightly points out, the problem then resolves itself into one of conflicting terminology and the question which remains to be answered is: Does this conclusion necessitate the restriction of the term State to those bodies politic that may properly be said to possess Sovereignty? This question Willoughby answers as follows: "If the terms State is to be regarded as a technical one, scientific accuracy would seem to demand that this be done, for, as has been seen, if it be employed in a sense that is in anywise broader, it becomes impossible to refuse to apply it to political units or organizations which political scientists in the past have never so dignified. Upon the other hand, if only those political entities are to be designated as States which are sovereign in character, common usage will be equally violated by excluding from its application many political units which have been almost universally so denominated. The only escape from these two alternatives, both of them highly objectionable should seem to be for the analytical jurist to abandon the effort to give scientific precision to the term State and to obtain accuracy of expression by qualifying it when necessary, with such adjectives as sovereign, non-sovereign and the like. If one were starting with a clear sheet, or essaying to formulate a scientifically exact terminology for the analytical jurist there can be little doubt that it would be wise to refuse to designate as States those political entities in which sovereignty does not inhere, but, as it is, with a wide but less precise usage practically universal, such a restriction is not practicable...."[2]

A similar confusion exists with regard to the use of the term Sovereignty as the legal will of the sovereign or independent State. The analytical jurist speaks of the State as possessing a will, ascribing to the State a function

[2] *Ibid.*, pp. 269-270.

borrowed from man viewed from the aspect of religion, philosophy and psychology. Religious, philosophical and psychological investigation is interested in the question of what willing means, how it is done, why we will or want to will, and whatever facts are obtainable concerning the cause and effect of the divergence of will power possessed by individual men. The jurist, on the other hand is interested only to determine whether and to what extent a certain individual political unit is endowed with a will as a legal competence to perform certain acts, to enjoy certain privileges, to possess certain goods or properties and to command obedience to its laws within definitely established degrees or limitations. The analytical jurist is not concerned over the question how the individual political unit secures the possession of that will or how it effects a change in the degree of the legal competence possessed by it. He merely considers the question of the actual possession of such a legal will and the degree of such competence. With regard to the Sovereignty or independence of such a unit he is interested merely in the question, whether the degree of this legal competence is such as to be equivalent to what political scientists and international jurists have agreed to call Sovereignty.

In the sphere of religion, philosophy and psychology we recognize an indefinite divergence of the degrees of man's will. In that sense we speak for instance of the difference of the will power of men as individuals. In the ascending scale of man's will considered as will power we speak of a master will as superior to other wills, but we do not attribute to any man an omnipotent will. In other words, we conceive and even attempt to measure the relative difference of man's will power, but we do not attempt to establish or find an individual possessed of a supreme, i. e. omnipotent will.

The same applies to the sphere of jurisprudence. Willing or being possessed of a will in the legal sense means having a certain definable or defined degree of legal competence to perform specific functions, to enjoy particular benefits, to possess a definite share of material goods, to be subject to certain restrictions and to observe certain obligations. In the case of the State considered as a juristic person, it means in addition to all this the enforcement of the State's legal norms upon its citizens and magistracy. It should be clear then that when the analytical jurist speaks of the will of a State or a political unit he refers to the legal competence of that particular unit to perform certain acts, to enjoy certain benefits or to assume certain obligations, to enforce obedience to its laws, and that when he speaks of States being possessed of different degrees of legal will, he must be taken to mean a difference of legal competence. Thus when the jurist says that a number of States possess a supreme legal will called Sovereignty he means that each of these States possesses a degree of legal competence which, under the prevailing definitions of international law and according to the present conception of political realities, entitle these political units to the status of independent or sovereign States. And when he says that a number of political units do not possess such Sovereignty he means that they lack that degree of legal competence. What varies is not Sovereignty, but the degree of legal competence serving as the criterion for the presence or absence of Sovereignty. This variation of the degree of legal competence is the result of political forces beyond the control of the analytical jurist. But it is on the basis of this variation that he classifies the political units in question as either possessing or as not possessing Sovereignty. From this it follows that the supreme legal will called Sovereignty as possessed by some States is conceived as a legal will superior to that of those political units not possessing Sovereignty and not as legal omnipotence in the sense in which the term has been applied by those who have taken exception to its use in this connection.

Confusion of Legal and Political Thinking. The difficulty of the problem here discussed is on the face of it one of a conflicting or ambiguous terminology. In the last analysis, however, it has its cause not in any fundamental shortcoming of the juristic conception of the State, but in the confusion of political and legal thinking on the part of those attempting to apply the theory without a clear understanding of the premises.

It is not and cannot be the object of the juristic theory of the State and Sovereignty to assign to certain bodies politic the character of States and to deny the same to others. To be more specific, it is not the task of the analytical jurist to apportion to some political organizations a sufficient degree of legal competency in order to justify their claim to statehood in the sense in which international law defines it, or to deprive other political units of such competencies in order to deny their claim to such a status. It is up to the individual body politic to prove the possession of such a degree of legal competence, or failing such possession, to acquire it in whatever way international law permits. The present succession States to the former Austro-Hungarian Empire secured the degree of legal competence considered indispensable under present-day prevailing international and constitutional law to their claim to independence and sovereign statehood. But the process by which they secured this competence was a purely political one, i. e., successful revolution terminating in the dissolution of the old federal bond holding them in the Sovereignty of the former Austro-Hungarian union, which up to that time alone was recognized by the Society of Nations as an independent or sovereign State. The analytical jurist had nothing to do with the procedure. He is interested merely in the fact that there are now so many more political units coming, as Laski puts it, within the four corners of the theory, a fact which naturally adds to its general applicability and acceptance.

On the other hand, the present succession States of the former Austro-Hungarian Empire, had, long before their successful revolution, while actually constituting more or less autonomous administrative units of that Empire, very pronounced aspirations to statehood. No doubt they had, especially Hungary, by political pressure gradually increased their legal competencies to a point where it was, in the mind of some of its more optimistic patriots, difficult to decide whether it was their own will which prevailed in the matter of their government or whether it was the will of the Empire. But as long as international politics and law did not recognize them as independent States, so long the analytical jurist could not be held to account for the fact that these political units did not come within the range of a definition of the State derived from what international actualities and political practice have decreed and what analytical jurisprudence has accepted, as independent and sovereign States.

The question may, of course, be asked, why the analytical jurist chose as his starting point this independent State instead of the political unit having all the earmarks of statehood but independence? The answer is that he could do nothing else if he was to conform to the realities of international politics and law. At the time when the juristic conception of the State asserted itself as the correct interpretation of modern State life and law, it was only the independent State which in the international legal sense was considered as possessing statehood. All other political units claiming such a status were in theory and practice denied the State character by the sovereign States whose legal and political supremacy they were constrained to acknowledge. As a matter of fact the same condition prevails to-day. Let us apply the argument used in the case of the succession States of the Austro-Hungarian Kaiserreich to the British Empire, the United States and the German Reich. Is it not a fact that the advocates of federalization in the British Empire and the States' righters in the United States and Germany insist upon the State character of their respective commonwealths not because they consider themselves in actual possession of that degree of legal competence equivalent to independence, but as a method of propaganda in the struggle towards the achievement of that status as is the case in the British Empire, and as a protest against the apparently irrevocable loss of that status in the United States and Germany?

The present succession States of the Austro-Hungarian Empire secured their present status as independent States by revolution. They had been preparing the ground for such achievement for decades preceding the war by more or less peaceful political pressure, by the process of evolution. It is this evolutionary rather than revolutionary method which seems to be at work in the dominions of the British Empire for the gradual emancipation from British Sovereignty. But with this process of gaining statehood the analytical jurist has no more to do than with that by revolutionary procedure. It is like the latter a purely political problem which concerns only the political units involved. The political philosopher or the analytical jurist is concerned merely with the question whether the constitutions of these political units recognize the final legally binding authority of the British Crown or the King in Parliament, or whether they reject such authority and prove the political efficacy of such rejection by securing the recognition of their political independence in international law.

As a matter of fact, most of the British dominions populated by western European stock and a few others such as Egypt, have acquired in some way or other many of the characteristics of the State in the juristic sense. They may thus be said to be in a state of transition to full statehood. But as long as they find it to their interest to acknowledge either voluntarily or under duress the legally and politically binding Sovereignty of the British Crown, or the British Parliament, they may claim to possess a varying and increasing degree of legal competency, but they still fall short of that degree needed for independence. Legally speaking they are not independent, sovereign States, though politically they may enjoy a status little different from that of other political units nominally claiming independence, but actually acknowledging a degree of servitudes amounting to an abridgment of their Sovereignty from a practical point of view.[3]

Political Pretensions versus Legal Facts. In the United States the Sovereignty of the Union was challenged by the seceding States in the Civil War, but it was definitely established as a political and legal fact by the

[3] According to the decision of the British Imperial Conference of 1926, the self-governing Dominions of the Empire have been declared "autonomous Communities within the British Empire, equal in status, in no way subordinate one to another in any aspect of their domestic or external affairs, though united by a common allegiance to the Crown, and freely associated as members of the British Commonwealth of Nations." The existence of this common allegiance to the Crown has not been affected by the Conference's practical concessions to the self-governing activities of the Dominions concerned, such as the curtail-

outcome of that war. In Germany the independence of the individual units of the Holy Roman Empire of the German Nation, specifically acknowledged in the formal dissolution of the Empire and in the Articles of affiliation of the German Federation of 1815, was definitely relinquished by the establishment of the North German Confederation of 1866 or 1867, succeeded in legal continuity by the Empire of 1871 and the National Republic of 1918. It is nevertheless true that in Germany the issue of the State character of the Länder is still a serious one. It dominates the political life of some of the most powerful commonwealths of the Reich to the detriment of National solidarity in the field of domestic and foreign relations. It prompts jurists of authoritative standing to posit the statehood of the body politic without the possession of independence as shown in chapter XI. But serious though this issue is, it shows, more clearly than it could be shown with reference to any other Federal Union, the utter hollowness of the issue inasmuch as it proves without doubt that the insistence upon the name of State and the possession of a residue of Sovereignty is not based upon legal facts but upon political pretensions.

This phase of the problem has been considered in some detail by the author in a previous work dealing with the constitutional relations of the German States to the National Republican Reich in connection with Bavaria's attempted nullification of the Law for the Protection of the

ment of the supervisory and controlling functions of the Governors General, the exchange of high envoys between Dominions and His Majesty's Government in Great Britain, the exchange of diplomatic representatives between Dominions and foreign powers, the extension of autonomous rights in the sphere of Legislation (For text of the Conference's Report see the Journal of Comparative Legislation and International Law, 3. Ser., vol. IX, pt. I, p. 68 ff.).

Republic of 1921.[4] In order to put an end to the assassination of prominent statesmen of a republican leaning the National President issued two ordinances later enacted as national law, penalizing the activities of certain secret societies, curtailing the right of public gathering and speech, etc. The Bavarian Government issued a counter ordinance nullifying certain provisions of the National law within Bavarian territory. Under Article 48 of the National Constitution the National President had the right to demand the repeal of the Bavarian ordinance and in case of a refusal on the part of Bavaria to employ the National forces to secure obedience to the National will. Considering the precarious situation of the Reich at the time, President Ebert secured the nominal repeal of the ordinance by a compromise between the National and Bavarian governments.

The legal status defining the relations of Reich and States on the point at issue was clear beyond doubt. This legal status permitted the enactment of the National Law in question under Article 48 of the National Constitution. The same legal status precluded the legal right on the part of Bavaria to nullify any provision of that law within Bavarian territory. Nevertheless, Bavaria did thus attempt nullification, and by a technical subterfuge even tried to justify its attempt at nullification on the basis of the same Article 48 of the National Constitution.[5]

This interpretation of the facts involved is substantiated in an article by Dr. Piloty, Professor of constitutional law

[4] Bavaria and the Reich, the Conflict over the Law for the Protection of the Republic.... The Johns Hopkins Press, 1923.

[5] Section 4 of Article 48 stipulates that in case of impending danger the government of a Land may within its territory take emergency measures. At the request of the National President or of the Reichstag these measures must be repealed.

at the University of Munich.[6] Piloty, defending the action of the Bavarian government as politically justified, nevertheless concedes that the National Constitution establishes the relations of the Reich and the component parts in such a way that there seems to be no room for controversy on that score, provided a legal view is taken. But he adds, a clear separation of the political and constitutional aspects of the conflict under discussion, was impossible so long as the conflict lasted. According to Piloty, the National Law for the Protection of the Republic constituted a political blunder of such magnitude that it necessitated the methods of political fight on the part of Bavaria. But on what score could the National law have been such a blunder? Did it transgress the National material, if not formal, constitutional competence and thus give to Bavaria the reciprocal right to fight in an extra-constitutional manner?

An answer to this and to all other questions involved, can, according to Piloty, be given only on the basis of a clear and unequivocal acceptance of the "Rechtsnatur des Reiches." This is possible only if we recognize the Constitution of Weimar as the supreme source of the law prevailing to-day.

Accepting the National Constitution of 1919 as the legal basis for the definition of the relations of Reich and Länder, Piloty reasons that the characterization of the Reich as Bundesstaat or as a federal structure does not serve to clarify these relations. "That the Reich from the aspect of its organization, competencies and the functioning of its government, is not a Bund but a Staat, is brought out much more definitely by the Constitution of Weimar than ....by that of 1871.... If Sovereignty, supreme power,

[6] Piloty, Der Streit zwischen Bayern und dem Reich über die Republikschutzgesetze und seine Lösung, in Archiv des öffentlichen Rechts, 43. bd., 3. hft., pp. 305-348.

is the essential of the State, as claimed by the correct doctrine, then the Reich alone is a State....and the Länder are not States." However, Piloty does not conceive of the Länder as provinces or communities of the Reich. They have, he declares, a certain degree of autonomy which places them above these categories. In all spheres of their State activity and power over which the Reich does not claim exclusive competency, they possess a residue of Hoheitsrechte. Within the bounds of these rights the States may move at their pleasure. Then, qualifying this statement, Piloty adds that, nevertheless, there are limits drawn for them by the sovereign German Reich as the superior political and sovereign power (Staatsgewalt). Thus "the German States constitute a special constitutional type, being neither province nor State, but simply Land, that is a kind of raised or exalted public law tribal association endowed with definite rights and kept in definite dependence by the will of the Reich and by the National Constitution." [7]

Thus, Piloty concedes as the present status the constitutional supremacy of the National Union over the German States. But he insists that the limitations placed upon the legal competency of the States "are not capable of final definition because the general interest of the Reich, that is, of the German people, cannot once for all be defined at one given time." In other words the present legal relations between Reich and States may be changed at a time when the interests of the Reich may demand such a change and consequently "the State character of the Länder, the term applied by Bavaria to the sum total of what is left to the Länder, is not an absolutely certain legal concept of unchangeable content."

[7] The preceding discussion and the quotation are taken more or less literally from the author's Bavaria and the Reich...., p. 88 ff.

Piloty's interpretation of the situation substantiates the argument advanced above in connection with the author's reference to the dominions of the British Empire and the former commonwealths of Austria-Hungary. At the present time, Piloty says, the German National union is the sovereign State, the Länder are dependent political organizations of some kind or other. Their present status he does not consider necessarily a final one. The interests of the Reich may at a future time demand a change in the relations of Reich and Länder affecting the status of the Länder in such a way that they will be recognized in constitutional and international law as independent States. But until this takes place, the fact remains that they are not States in the international legal sense and therefore cannot claim Statehood and Sovereignty under the juristic conception of the State.

Once more it must be said, however, that such a change, if or when it takes place, will be effected not by the extension of the juristic conception of the State to the new independent States but by a political act on the part of the political units concerned, the consequences of which will bring them into the category of States within the operation of analytical jurisprudence.

From the preceding considerations it must appear that the claim to statehood and to a residue of Sovereignty on the part of dependent political units has no foundation from the strictly legal point of view. It has its raison d'être in political grievances or ambitions. But while this realization does not eliminate the difficulty of terminology it has at least clarified the issue in one respect. It has established the fact that the fault does not lie with the juristic conception of the State, but with those, be they jurists or statesmen, who place a purely political thought content into purely juristic terms. As long as international law and political reality insist upon the formal recognition of independence as the criterion of full statehood in the juristic sense, so long the analytical jurist need not concern himself over the fact that statesmen and politicians erroneously apply the term State and Sovereignty to certain political units regardless of their actual legal status. The analytical jurist need not be concerned over his position until international law and political reality have come to the point of conceding that independence in the sense in which it is defined to-day, exists only in theory but not in fact and that what counts in the life of political units is the definite establishment and demarkation of their respective legal competencies, vary as they may in each case, rather than the possession or non-possession of that particular degree considered equivalent to Sovereignty. Whether this will or will not come about or whether it is already near at hand is purely a question of opinion or politics, not one of jurisprudence.[8]

[8] A most convincing argument in favor of this contention is found in Edward J. Pheelan's recent article "The Sovereignty of the Irish Free State." In this article the writer puts the question: "Is the Irish Free State a full international person, or what is frequently called a 'sovereign State'?" Enumerating and analyzing the legal competencies of the Irish Free State he summarizes them as follows: "We have seen that the Irish Free State possesses the right of Legation and the treaty making power. Therefore she has the ability required. Her right to use it has been recognized by the formal decision of the League of Nations. Her special relationship with the other Members of the British Commonwealth of Nations we have seen does not alter the status which is thus hers. She has been admitted 'to join in a solemn Covenant to exercise the powers of her sovereign status in promoting the peace, security and happiness, the economic and cultural well-being of the human races'." On the basis of this summary he concludes that: "She could devote her 'sovereignty' to no higher ideal, and its extent can best be defined by her recognized share in those supreme responsibilities, participation in which is the essential mark of modern Statehood" (Review of Nations, March, 1927).

CONCLUSION

Resumé and Finale

In conclusion we must bring back to our mind the object of this work as set forth in the preface and introduction. As stated in the preface the study here offered was undertaken in connection with a series of studies of the new European Constitutions. It was natural then that prior to the examination of these constitutions the attempt should be made to arrive at a clear understanding as to the meaning of the terminology most essential to the proper treatment of the subject. This attempt necessitated a broad review and analysis of the theories of State, Sovereignty and Law advanced by the political thinkers of the past and present. The first constitution approached by the author was that of the German National Republic. This was found to be obviously and ostensibly based on the juristic conception of the State. It was equally natural, then, that the juristic conception of the State, having thus found practical demonstration of its applicability to the modern State, but being nevertheless rejected as an antiquated myth or a dangerous fallacy by some prominent present-day political writers and jurists, should demand the author's special attention. The object of the preceding chapters has therefore been in the first place to find a theory of the State and Sovereignty so broad and simple that it may be applied consistently to all existing politically organized societies; in the second place, to examine for this purpose the most important theories of the past and present with regard to such applicability; and in the third place to examine in a judicial manner on the one hand, the claim of the advocates of the juristic conception of the State that it is their theory which alone is suitable to the modern concept of law, State and international realities, and on the other hand the criticism of its opponents to the effect that it is anything but that.

In the course of the analysis of the most prominent doctrines of State and Sovereignty we started out with the theory of Sovereignty elaborated by Bodin, defining Sovereignty as the supreme will and power of the prince or king as the representative and agent of God, to whom alone he owes an accounting for his governance. Stressing the idea of the supremacy of the National or central ruler over the decentralized feudal system of the middle ages, Bodin's theory must be acknowledged to constitute the first step in the direction of central or National authority bringing order out of the chaos of a multitude of conflicting claimants to the same position and the same authority. But to the extent to which he limited the possession of that Sovereignty to the monarch, he precluded the general application of his theory to those political units where the National ruler did not succeed in securing or in maintaining the position assigned to him by Bodin.

The more modern compact or contract theory, which has been shown to be a cross between the Roman idea of the people's complete surrender of its original right of self governance to the ruler and the feudal concept of the conditional contract between lord and vassal, made a permanent breach in the doctrine of the divine right of the sovereign prince or king. If the ruler, sovereign though he claimed to be, was bound to rule justly and benevolently, if in other words he was subject to some kind of law, be it divine law, or natural law as part of divine law, then his governance was, despite his own allegation to the contrary, subject to control by those who could enforce the divine or natural law against princes or kings. Those who thus first enforced this law against self willed kings and emperors were the popes, claiming the right to interpret and administer that law for the benefit of universal Christendom. They enforced the law as need arose by absolving a whole people or nation from its allegiance to king or emperor. But without the cooperation on the part of the ruler's subjects even the Pope would have been powerless to bring a king to terms. Hence it was after all not the Pope, but the people who as the force behind the Pope's dictum forced their rulers to acknowledge a will superior to their (the rulers') own.

Here somebody shrewdly discovered the germ of national Sovereignty as a doctrine diametrically opposed to that of the Sovereignty of the monarch who with Louis XIV would say "L'état c'est moi." The doctrine of nationl Sovereignty was solemnly proclaimed by revolutionary France not as a theory but as a reality. As applied in France it implied also the Sovereignty of the Nation as opposed to the assertion of Sovereignty by any part of the Nation. In this interpretation it was the guiding principle in the constitutional development of the American Union. In the same interpretation it has been playing the same rôle in the unification of the Italian States and in the final abandonment by the German States of their claim of political independence from whatever federal or national ties held them in the form of Empire, Bund or Reich.

In the resentment of the extremists of the French Revolution against the autocratic rule of the Monarchy this idea of national Sovereignty of the French State as distinguished from and set up against that of the king, soon became the slogan of popular Sovereignty or supremacy of the unrestricted will of the people contrasted with any governing agency, king, or what not, embodying elimination and death not only for kings and rulers but threatening destruction to State and Society.

Teaching the sanctity of the law as the will of the State formulated by the constitutionally designated legislature and the irrestible character of the executive as the executor of that law, both Kant and Hegel rendered an essential service to political theory and practice in the direction of the modern idea of the Rechtsnatur of the State. Stressing the necessity for the establishment of some kind of control of the ruling agent of the State Fichte brought into profile the essential difference between State and Government as the basic elements of the juristic conception of the State, a difference unfortunately so little understood or recognized by the critics of that theory.

Starting with a critical analysis of law as the foundation of his theory of Sovereignty, Austin finally laid the cornerstone for the structure of the juristic conception of the State and Sovereignty as developed by Willoughby. As demonstrated in its present interpretation and restatement this conception demands recognition as the only doctrine applicable to the modern State, provided of course that we can agree on a definition of the modern State satisfactory alike to adherent and critic of the theory.

Speaking in the language of the jurist it seems fair to say that the modern definition of the State has been fixed by the realities of politics and international law. Thinking in the terms of the statesman or politician we may assert that the concept of the State is still in the making, that the definition satisfying the jurist is an erroneous one and that consequently the juristic conception of the State based upon that definition is not tenable.

Finally pondering over the most recent doctrine positing the supremacy of international over municipal law, or asserting the State character of the body politic regardless of independence in international law, a doctrine fortuitously synchronized by the establishment of a League of Nations as a promising enterprise in the direction of the realization of these doctrines, we may feel inclined to suspend our own judgment as to the tenability and the extent of the applicability of the juristic conception of the State.

Concerning the author's position with regard to these three possibilities and concerning his conviction the reader can hardly be left in doubt. Whether the reader agrees with that position and shares that conviction matters not. The object of this study is not to win converts to a particular view or opinion. It has been no more or less than to examine for the author's own peace of mind in a manner as judicial as possible the premises involved. The result of his examination he offers with the hope of stimulating independent thinking, contributing thereby to the eventual emergence of a Society of Nations whose members will look towards the definition and recognition of their legal competencies as an opportunity for greater cooperation in the direction of peaceful international relations rather than a chance to establish or enhance their individual status as sovereign or independent States.

BIBLIOGRAPHY

Anschütz, Gerhard, Deutsches Staatsrecht (Holtzendorff's Enzyklopädie der Rechtswissenschaft....vol. IV, 1914).

———, Die Verfassung des Deutschen Reichs vom 11. August 1919....Berlin, G. Stilke, 1921.

Austin, John, The Austinian Theory of Law, being an edition of lectures I, V, and VI of Austin's Jurisprudence and of Austin's "Essay on the uses of the Study of Jurisprudence...." by W. Jethro Brown....London, J. Murray, 1906.

Bodin, Les Six livres de la République....à Genève, par Etienne Gamonet, 1629.

Bullowa, Ferd. E. M., The History of the Theory of Sovereignty.... New York, W. R. Jenkins, 1895.

Coker, Francis W., The Technique of the Pluralistic State (American Political Science Review, vol. XV, 1921, p. 186 ff).

Corpus Juris Civilis, Institutiones, Imp. Justiniani Institutionum libri quattuor, cum praefatione et ex recognitione Eduardi Huschke, Lipsiae, B. G. Teubner, 1868.

Crane, Robert T., Discussion [of Willoughby's The Juristic Conception of the State] (The American Political Science Review, vol. XII, 1918, pp. 209-214).

Dicey, Albert Venn, Introduction to the Study of the Law of the Constitution....8. ed., London, MacMillan and Co., 1915.

Duguit, Léon, Le droit social, le droit individuel et la transformation de l'état, Paris, F. Alcan, 1908.

———, The Law and the State. French and German Doctrines ....tr. by F. J. de Sloovère (Harvard Law Review, vol. XXXI, 1917, no. 1).

———, Law in the Modern State....tr. by Frida and Harold Laski, New York, B. W. Huebsch, 1919.

———, Les transformations du droit public....Paris, Librarie Armand Colin, 1913.

Ellis, Elleen Deborah, Political Science at the Crossroads (American Political Science Review, vol. XXI, 1927, pp. 773-791).

Esmein, A., Eléments de Droit constitutionnel français et comparé.... 6. ed., Paris, Librarie de la Société du Récueil Sirey, 1914.

Fichte, Johann Gottlieb, Beiträge zur Berichtigung der Urtheile des Publicums über die französische Revolution (....Sämmtl. Werke......vol. VI).

———, Der geschlossene Handelsstaat....(....Sämmtl. Werke ....vol. III).

————, Grundlage des Naturrechts....(....Sämmtl. Werke.... vol. III).

————, Reden an die deutsche Nation....(....Sämmtl. Werke.... vol. VII)

————, Das System der Sittenlehre....(....Sämmtl. Werke.... vol. IV).

————, Zurückforderung der Denkfreiheit von den Fürsten Europens, die sie bisher unterdrückten....Eine Rede.... (....Sämmtl. Werke....hrsg. von J. H. Fichte, Berlin, Verlag von Veit und com., vol. VI).

Figgis, John N., Studies of Political Thought from Gerson to Grotius, 1414-1625....Cambridge, The University Press, 1907.

————, The Theory of the Divine Right of Kings....Cambridge, The University Press, 1896.

Follett, M. P., The New State, Group Organization, the Solution of Popular Government....Longmans, Green and Co....1918.

Gaius, Gai Institutiones or Institutes of Roman Law by Gaius. With translation and commentary by the late Edward Poste.... Oxford, Clarendon Press, 1904.

Garner, James W., Limitations on National Sovereignty in International Relations (The American Political Science Review, vol. XIX, 1925, pp. 1-24).

Gierke, Otto F., Das deutsche Genossenschaftsrecht....Berlin, Weidmann, 1868-1913.

————, Political Theories of the Middle Ages....tr. by....Maitland, Cambridge, The University Press, 1913.

Hatschek, Julius, Deutsches und preussisches Staatsrecht....Berlin, Verlag von Georg Stilke, 1922-3.

Hegel, Georg Wilhelm Friederich, Grundlinien der Philosophie des Rechts (....Werke. Vollständige Ausgabe....Berlin, Duncker und Humblot, 1832-40, vol. VIII).

Henrich, Walter, Das Sollen als Grundlage der Rechtswissenschaft (Zeitschrift für öffentliches Recht, vol. II, 1921, p. 131 ff.).

————, Theorie des Staatsgebietes, entwickelt aus der Lehre von den lokalen Kompetenzen der Staatsperson....Wien, Leipzig, G. Freytag, 1922.

————, Zur Theorie der Rechtskraft (Archiv des öffentlichen Rechts....N. F., 7. Bd., 1924, pp. 329-350).

Hobbes, Thomas, Leviathan, or the Matter, Form and Power of a Commonwealth, Ecclesiastical and Civil, with an introduction by Henry Morley....London, New York, G. Routledge and Sons, 1885.

————, Elementa philosophica de cive....Amsterodami, apud H. et viduam Th. Boom, 1696.

Hooker, Richard, Of the Laws of Ecclesiastical Polity....London, J. M. Dent & Co., 1907.

Jellinek, Walter, Revolution und Reichsverfassung....(Jahrbuch des öffentlichen Rechts, vol. IX).

Justinianus, Institutiones, see Corpus Juris Civilis, Institutiones.

Kaltenborn von Stachau, Karl, Kritik des Völkerrechts....Leipzig, 1847.

Kant, Immanuel, The Philosophy of Law. An exposition of the fundamental principles of jurisprudence as the Science of Right ....tr. from the German by W. Hastie....Edinburgh, T. & T. Clark, 1887.

Kelsen, Hans, Allgemeine Staatslehre....Berlin, J. Springer, 1925.

———, Gott und Staat (Logos, bd. XI, 1922-23, hft. 3-4).

———, Hauptprobleme der Staatsrechtslehre, entwickelt aus der Lehre vom Rechtssatze....Tübingen, J. C. B. Mohr, 1911.

———, ———, 2. Aufl., 1923.

———, Das Problem der Souveränität und die Theorie des Völkerrechts....Tübingen, J. C. B. Mohr, 1920.

———, Rechtswissenschaft und Recht. Erledigung der Rechtsdogmatik (Zeitschrift für öffentliches Recht, vol. III, 1922-23, p. 103 ff.).

———, Sozialismus und Staat, eine Untersuchung der politischen Theorie des Marxismus....2 Aufl., Leipzig, C. L. Hirschfeld, 1923.

———, Der soziologische und der juristische Staatsbegriff.... Tübingen, J. C. B. Mohr, 1922.

———, Das Verhältnis von Staat und Recht im Lichte der Erkenntnistheorie (Zeitschrift für öffentliches Recht....vol. II, 1921, p. 453 ff.).

———, Zur Lehre vom öffentlichen Rechtsgeschäft (Archiv des öffentlichen Rechts, vol. 31, p. 247 ff.).

Krabbe, H., The Modern Idea of the State....tr. by G. H. Sabine and W. J. Shepard....New York, London, D. Appelton, and Co., 1922.

Kunz, Josef L., On the Theoretical Basis of the Law of Nations (The Grotius Society. London. Transactions, vol. 10, 1925, pp. 115-142).

———, Völkerrechtswissenschaft und reine Rechtslehre....Wien, Deuticke Verlag, 1923.

Laski, Harold Joseph, Authority in the Modern State....New Haven, Yale University Press, 1919.

———, The Foundations of Sovereignty and other Essays....New York, Harcourt, Brace and Co., 1921.

———, A Grammar of Politics....London, G. Allen & Unwin, 1925.

———, A Note on Duguit (Harvard Law Review, vol. XXXI, 1917, no. 1, pp. 186-192).

———, [Review of Willoughby's The Fundamental Concepts of Public Law] Political Science Quarterly, vol. XL, 1925, no. 4, pp. 618-621).

———, Studies in the Problem of Sovereignty....New Haven, Yale University Press, 1917.

Lenz, Georg, Autorität und Demokratie in der Staatslehre des Hans Kelsen (Schmollers Jahrbuch, 50. Jahrg., 1926, pp. 589-621).

———, Zur Rechtfertigung des Staates (Schmollers Jahrbuch, 49. Jahrg., 1925, pp. 221-230).

Lieber, Francis, Manual of Political Ethics, designed chiefly for the use of Colleges and Students at Law....2. ed....Philadelphia, J. B. Lippincott & Co., 1875.

Locke, John, Two Treatises on Civil Government....preceded by Sir Robert Filmer's "Patriarcha," with an introduction by Henry Morley....London, New York, G. Routledge & Sons, 1884.

Maine, Sir Henry, Ancient Law....New York, Henry Holt and Co., 1906.

Malberg, R. Carré de, Contribution à la théorie générale de l'Etat, spécialement d'après les données fournies par le droit constitutionnel français....Paris, Librairie de la Société du Recueil Sirey, 1920-22.

Meyer, Georg,....Lehrbuch des deutschen Staatsrechts....7. Aufl. bearb. von Gerhard Anschütz....München und Leipzig, Duncker & Humblot, 1919.

Nelson, Leonard, Die Rechtswissenschaft ohne Recht. Kritische Betrachtungen über die Grundlagen des Staats- und Völkerrechts, insbesondere über die Lehre von der Souveränetät....Leipzig, Verlag von Viet & Co., 1917.

Olsson, Gustaf, Det Statsrealistiska problemet till den rättsfilosofiska skolan i Wien....Lund, Gleenupska Universitets-bokhandeln, 1925.

Pheelan, Edward J., The Sovereignty of the Irish Free State (Review of Nations, March, 1927).

Potter, Pitman B., An Introduction to the Study of International Organization....New York, The Century Co., 1925.

Rousseau, Jean Jacques, A dissertation on political economy; to which is added a treatise on the social compact; or the Principles of politic law....1. American edition, Comp. from the works of the author, Albany, Barber & Southwick, 1797.

Sander, Fritz, Rechtsdogmatic oder Theorie der Rechtserfahrung (Zeitschrift für öffentliches Recht, vol. II, 1921, p. 511 ff.).

Schmitt-Dorotić, Carl, Die Diktatur. Von den Anfängen des modernen Souveränitätsgedankens bis zum proletarischen Klassenkampf....München, Duncker & Humblot, 1921.

——————, Politische Theologie; vier Kapitel zur Lehre von der Souveränität....München, Duncker & Humblot, 1922.

Solière, Eug., Le Plébiscite dans l'annexion. Etude historique et critique de droit des gens....Paris, L. Boyer, 1901.

Verdross, Alfred, Die Einheit des rechtlichen Weltbildes auf Grundlage der Völkerrechtsverfassung....Tübingen, J. C. B. Mohr, 1923.

——————, Grundlagen und Grundlegungen des Völkerrechts (Zeitschrift für internationales Recht., vol. 29, p. 65 ff.).

——————, Völkerrecht und ein einheitliches Rechtssystem. Kritische Studie zu den Völkerrechtstheorien von Max Wenzel, Hans Kelsen und Fritz Sander (Zeitschrift für Völkerrecht, XII. bd., 1923, pp. 405-438).

Vinogradoff, Sir Paul, The Juridical Nature of the State (Michigan Law Review, vol. XXIII, 1924, pp. 138-153).

Watkins, R. Dorsey, The State as a Party Litigant....Baltimore, Johns Hopkins Press, 1927.

Weber, Alfred, Die Krise des modernen Staatsgedankens in Europa.... Berlin und Leipzig, Deutsche Verlags-anstalt Stuttgart, 1925.

Willoughby, W. W., An Examination of the Nature of the State. A Study in Political Philosophy....New York and London, MacMillan & Co., 1906 and 1911.

——————, The Fundamental Concepts of Public Law....New York, The Macmillan Co., 1924.

——————, The Juristic Conception of the State (The American Political Science Review, vol. XII, 1918, pp. 192-208).

——————, The Political Theories of the Ancient World....New York, London, Longmans, Green & Co., 1903.

Wolff, Christian, Grundsätze des Natur- und Völckerrechts....Halle, Rengerische buchhandlung, 1754.

Wolzendorff, Kurt, Der reine Staat. Skizze zum Problem einer neuen Staatsepoche (Zeitschrift für die gesamte Staatswissenschaft, 75. Jahrg., 1920, pp. 199-229).

——————, Staatsrecht und Naturrecht in der Lehre vom Widerstandsrecht des Volkes gegen rechtswidrige Ausübung der Staatsgewalt; zugleich ein Beitrag zur Entwicklungsgeschichte des modernen Staatsgedankens....Breslau, M. & H. Marcus, 1916.

INDEX

www.ingramcontent.com/pod-product-compliance
Lightning Source LLC
LaVergne TN
LVHW101502200926
848483LV00001B/195
* 9 7 8 1 5 8 4 7 7 9 1 8 6 *